"Well written, enlightening, and a story that *must* be told."

—*Patricia S. Casey, former administrative assistant for Dr. Maya Angelou*

"Julia Torres relays a powerful and transparent story with a writing style that grips the reader to want to know more. It's a life story everyone can relate and identify with at some level. It will touch your heart and cause you to both feel the anguish and joy as you are taken on a journey of joy, heartache, and faith. A journey that will inevitably cause you to think about your own journey of faith and hope."

—*Steve Hannett, Jesus Reigns International, President and Founder, Abundant Grace Christian Church, Pastor*

"Julia Torres: one very strong woman, one amazing inspiration to us all!"

—*James A. Quattrochi, Director, Producer, Actor*

"For those who have experienced pain, this book will inspire you to realize how important it is to speak up and not suffer in silence. This is an exceptional story of how Torres turned tragedy into triumph. She unveils sexual abuse in the military and accurately depicts situations which lead up to the abuse occurring. A well-written book that immediately captured my attention. Julia, I applaud your bravery and can't wait to read more."

—*Dana Robinson-Street, Doctor of Nursing Practice, Family Nurse Practitioner-Board Certified, Health Professional Educator, Lieutenant, U.S. Navy, Retired*

"Julia Torres is a fighter—from playground battles in New Jersey, to Operation Desert Shield, from battling the effects of a date-rape drug to government-ordered BP pills silently waging war on her body. This is the explosive story of a young woman who never backs down, whether a decorated soldier bringing to light the cover-up of sexual harassment in the armed forces or later working as an undercover agent. As a high school and college English/Theatre teacher for forty-seven years, I recommend this brave, jaw-dropping book that chronicles the experiences of a true hero for readers 14 to 94."

—*Sarah Rosenberg, Co-Founder and Artistic Director of Open Hydrant Theatre Company, Bronx, New York*

"In her memoir, Julia Torres vividly and candidly invites us to share intimate moments which shaped her into the woman she is today, still standing. Her personal account of perseverance and triumph reminds us that our circumstances do not define us but rather mold us into the best version of ourselves."

—*Patty Smith, Lieutenant Colonel, U.S. Army*

# STILL STANDING

# STILL STANDING

*The Story of My Wars*

## JULIA TORRES

*Full Court Press*
*Englewood Cliffs, New Jersey*

*First Edition*

Copyright © 2014 by Julia Torres

Published in the United States of America
by Full Court Press, 601 Palisade Avenue
Englewood Cliffs, NJ 07632
www.fullcourtpressnj.com

Contact the author at JuliaTorresStillStanding@gmail.com

ISBN 978-1-938812-40-8
Library of Congress Control No. 2014958120

*Editing by Barry Sheinkopf, Maria Arriola-Fernandez,
and Patricia S. Casey*
*Book Design by Barry Sheinkopf for Bookshapers (www.bookshapers.com)*
*Cover art and photo enhancements by Rolando E. Corujo*
*Colophon by Liz Sedlack*

To Abuela, my giant

*For the sake of the silent*

IN MEMORY OF
*all the veterans, friends, and family
who went before me*

"Before I formed you in the womb
I knew you,
before you were born I set you apart."
—*Jeremiah* 1:5 (NIV)

*My first birthday, Havana, Cuba, April 6, 1968*

# *1*

# Friend or Foe

"JULIA, TRICIA WANTS TO FIGHT YOU after school," Jeanette said.

"Okay." I was confused about what I could possibly have done, but in seventh grade, you don't have to *do* anything to make a female classmate dislike you. Girls are catty creatures, and if one chooses not to like you, others will soon follow.

Tricia Thomas, one of the few Caucasian students and the most popular girl in seventh grade, wanted to fight me. I was popular but not mean.

Until then, I had never had a fist fight in Thomas Alva Edison Grammar School in Union City, New Jersey, an urban district nicknamed "Embroidery Capital of the World," known for its diverse immigrant culture and vast number of factory jobs.

Mom always taught us to avoid hostility; she did not like

confrontation and preferred to walk away from all aggression. In that respect, we were opposites and often locked heads.

Not heeding my mother's advice, I met Tricia after school. As a crowd of kids surrounded us a block away from the schoolyard that lovely spring day in 1980, I faced her and asked, "I'll fight you, but can you tell me why we're fighting?"

"Because I think you're conceited," she replied.

"I think that's a pretty stupid reason, but if that's what you want, okay."

I never cared too much about popular opinion. If I had, my life might have turned out differently, though not necessarily better. But I had my pride and did not want to give a false impression of fear.

Standing in front of a chain-link fence as Tricia removed her jacket, I wondered why I was even waiting. I moved forward and shoved her off the curb, causing her glasses to fall. The next thing I remember were fists flying. She punched my face, and I punched her stomach.

Shortly thereafter, the school librarian came up the block and stopped the fight. Bystanders vanished, and my dear friend Miguel looked at me with concern on his face. "I'll walk you home."

I wondered how I was going to break the news to Mom.

My mother did an outstanding job as a single parent. She gave us sensible advice when we were children, but as I grew older, I seldom followed it, finding her old-fashioned ways limiting and frustrating. Regardless, I loved and respected her.

When I entered our apartment, I sat on one of the floral-cushioned chairs at the kitchen table. The aroma of the previous night's meal lingered in the air, but as tasty as it had been then, it made knots in my stomach. In silent reflection, I waited for Mom to arrive, not mindful of the sun shining through the window.

A short while later, I heard her heavy footsteps coming up the stairs and began to get nervous. By the time the key turned in the lock, I had decided there was no easy explanation.

She entered, looked at me, and instinctively knew something was wrong. "What happened?"

"I got into a fight after school."

"Why? I didn't raise you to fight on the streets!" she muttered.

"I didn't have a choice."

"Why not?"

"Because I wasn't going to come off scared."

She dropped the conversation. Whether or not she agreed with me didn't matter at that moment, but her decision to accept my reason for defending myself did.

Diana Camacho, a girl who lived across the street, rang my bell within the hour. "Good fight, Julia. Tricia says she wants to fight you again tomorrow."

"Okay," I replied and went back upstairs.

In that instant, I realized something important—although I would not start a fight, I would not step down when threatened. Later that night on the phone, my best buddy Mara and I paired off our friends to fight Tricia's friends the following day, in case others jumped in.

But when I got to school the next morning, Tricia and I were summoned to the principal's office.

"Girls, please sit down," he said.

Mr. Bradshaw's office was not intimidating, and neither

was he. When we lined up in the schoolyard every morning, he welcomed us with a smile amid the noise and laughter. His shiny walnut desk, with a blank calendar in the center, a black-and-white analog clock on the left, and a telephone on the right, was as neat as his appearance. It was no surprise that he ran the school in the same organized fashion.

With disappointed determination, he began to speak in a low, clipped voice. "I received a telephone call early this morning from an anonymous caller who revealed that a gang fight would take place after school. The two of you were named as the ringleaders. I hope the caller was mistaken. You girls should be getting along—not fighting." He turned to me and asked, "Why would you want to fight?"

"Don't look at me. It wasn't my idea. Ask her," I snapped. *Why would he think I'd started it?*

Mom's words came to mind: "Immigrants and children of divorced parents are always the ones to blame when something goes wrong."

"Tricia?"

She shrugged. "I just don't like her. I think she's conceited."

"Tricia, are you familiar with the peacock?"

She shook her head.

"The peacock is an animal that prances around showing its beautiful plumage, but if it weren't for its feathers, the bird would have nothing."

His explanation did not make any sense to me. I thought that I was being compared to the peacock, and that he was wrong. But raised to respect authority, I remained quiet. So did Tricia.

"I'd like the two of you to promise me that there won't be any more fights after school. I'd like you to shake hands as a gesture of friendship."

"Okay," we said simultaneously, and did as he asked.

"Now go back to class."

That was the end of the alleged gang fight, but not the end of the alienation process. Giving your word and shaking hands must not have had the same meaning for Tricia as it did for me. She convinced all my girl friends to discontinue our friendships. Although it was disappointing to see my friends turn against me, the loss of my kindergarten friend Mara hurt me the most.

I gained a valuable lesson that year. My male friends, Miguel, Bruno, and Jesus, demonstrated the loyal strength of platonic male relationships that has enabled me to maintain close friendships with men of different ages today—something I wouldn't trade.

A year later, we were all looking forward to graduating from eighth grade. I thought the worst was over when Tricia came to me one day with a smirk on her face. "Marisol wants to talk to you after school."

Marisol, a member of a local female gang, was a tough, muscular seventh grader who'd transferred to our school from the Bronx. Rumor had it that she fought with knives.

Kids knew talking meant a fight would follow. She was no Tricia, and I wondered how I would get through it without getting my ass kicked badly.

"Who's Marisol?" I asked, knowing very well who she was.

"Freddy's sister," she replied, widening her grin.

I knew Freddy; he was the cutest boy in our grade. "What about?"

She shrugged, and I walked away pretending not to be concerned.

My stomach remained twisted for the rest of the day. By the time the dismissal bell rang, our interchange had spread across the school, bringing an even bigger crowd.

Miguel, Bruno, and Jesus, stood behind me as I faced Marisol.

She got right to the point. "I saw your name on the cheerleading team list."

"Yeah?"

"I wanna know why you made the team and I didn't. You didn't try out."

"I couldn't. I hurt my back, and I was already on the team last year." *So that's what this is about.* Marisol did not know I had been grandfathered onto the team.

"I want you to quit the team tomorrow. If you don't, we'll fight, and if you tell Mr. Bradshaw," she threatened, tapping her right index finger on my breastbone, "I'll kill you."

We kept looking at each other for a few seconds. When I didn't respond, she and the crowd scattered. I walked away with Miguel, Bruno, and Jesus.

"What are you gonna do?" asked Bruno.

"I dunno." I was doomed.

"You gonna quit the team?" Miguel asked.

"No," I replied.

"We don't wanna fight her brothers," said Jesus, the nervousness in his eyes evident behind prescription glasses.

Aside from Freddy, Marisol had two older brothers; all

three of them were members of a local male gang. They had rugged good looks and an innate toughness. This was appealing to the girls, but not to the guys who had to fight them.

Miguel, Bruno, and Jesus were not fighters unless they had to be. They were kids from good families who had been taught to defend an injustice but not to start trouble. Accustomed to fighting on the street, each of the brothers had a reputation for being just as tough as the others, and my friends were worried.

Bruno walked me the rest of the way home; then we parted. I watched him shuffle off with his hands in his pockets and wondered how I would handle the problem. Not wanting to see the boys or myself hurt, my head began to spin. One thing I knew for certain—no threat would make me quit the team.

And then an idea occurred to me that required Mom's help as well as that of the police. When she got home from work that evening, I told her what had happened and asked her to come with me to the police station the following morning.

Instead of going to school, we went to the Union City Police Department and spoke with detectives who advised me to be absent for the remainder of that day; in the interim, they would speak with Mr. Bradshaw, Marisol, and everyone else.

When I returned to school the next morning, the bullying had stopped. The girls had been warned to stay away from me or wind up in juvenile detention. I was relieved.

In the '70s, bullying did not receive as much attention as it does today. State and school laws are now ensuring that it is prevented, an approach that should have been adopted decades ago. Bullying has more than verbal or physical consequences; a victim can commit suicide—a growing trend.

Good things came from the experiences, though. Years later, Mara and I reconnected. After she apologized, we became friends again.

As for Tricia, I found her on Facebook one day and sent her a private message. *Hi, Tricia. Now that we are in our forties, can you tell me why you were so mean to me?*

She responded the next day. *I don't know. I felt guilty about it for many years.* I was hoping for a better answer, but I accepted it.

I am content with the way I handled adversity and harassment, experiences which seem pretty trivial compared to the harsher ones I encountered later in life.

# 2

# Inner City Princess

FORTUNATELY, THE LAST COUPLE OF YEARS as an Edison Eagle weren't all about peer conflicts.

During eighth grade I made a new best friend who, like me, sang alto in the school choir. One day after rehearsal I turned to Marissa. "You wanna get Chinese across the street?"

"Sure," she responded with her warm smile and soft brown eyes. Having lunch meant we'd buy pork-fried rice for a dollar at the corner store. Afterward, Marissa and I would sit on nearby doorsteps, dig into the white cartons, sip RC Colas, and chat until the school bell rang.

Our friendship blossomed as we laughed about the silly things kids found funny, such as the fart sounds that wet sneakers made in the classroom, and the older teacher who swore he was a stud. We spoke of our princess dreams to marry and live happily ever after and of our future professions—she wanted to be a pediatrician, and I a schoolteacher. From our teenage to adult years, Marissa and I crossed many milestones together, one in particular during our first summer as friends.

We were sitting on the floor of her parents' bedroom playing with Barbie dolls one afternoon, while her mom was in the kitchen preparing ham and cheese sandwiches, when the doorbell rang. Minutes later, the bedroom door creaked and Marissa's mom said, "Robert's here." Her cute, fourteen-year-old cousin had come to visit.

"Yikes!" screamed Marissa.

"Hurry up! Open the closet," I said in desperation.

Throwing the Barbies in a box with a loud thump, we tidied ourselves and left the room, closing the door of our childhood behind us.

We spent the remaining months eating at Summit Pizza in Union City, catching the bus with the boys to downtown Jersey City to watch a matinée movie, or climbing out of my kitchen window onto the neighboring rooftop we called Tar Beach, where we'd listen to radio music, dab on Coppertone, and lie on beach towels.

No matter what we did, there was never a dull moment, rather the usual teenage things—magazines, gossip, incessant laughter, and crushes. As young girls, we weathered the best and worst of times.

In fifth grade, the buzz through the school halls was that we had a cute new sixth-grader. I was curious to see if it was true until the following day, when the thud of a ball falling behind me in the noisy schoolyard made me turn. As the boy picked it up, our eyes met. We froze and were smitten.

He broke from the spell first, moving the handball from one hand to the other. "Hi, I'm Rudy. I'm new here."

His low, clear voice was music to my ears. With shaggy blond hair and glimmering hazel eyes, Rudy became my prince, and I, with long dark straight hair and ebony eyes, became his princess.

"Hi," I managed to say, clasping my hands together.

"You in sixth grade?" he asked.

"No, fifth."

"Oh. So is my sister, Mayra. You know her?"

"Not yet." My next thought hadn't been completely processed when the school bell rang. *Ugh!*

My budding prince dashed off to the other side of the castle. "See you later," he called out as he sped away. *I hope so!*

My wish came true. For two years, we flirted, enjoying each other's company and sharing laughter. The mere sight of his trying-to-be-cool attitude brought me giggles and blushes. We shared a fairy-tale kind of love in the magical way only kids can.

On May 6, 1981, a date forever engraved in my mind, the dismissal bell rang. I hurried out the door through a crowd of rowdy seventh-graders, welcoming the warm sunshine on my face. Everyone was happy to be out of school, but I was the happiest.

Rudy stood waiting for me, and I could've squealed with delight, swearing that I was the luckiest girl alive. For a few weeks, he had been meeting me after school, walking me home and carrying my books. The streets had never been long enough.

"How was school today?" he asked as he took my books.

My skin tingled when our hands briefly touched. "Good. How 'bout you?" I replied, as we began our stroll.

"Good." He smiled that half-smile that I found so endearing, but he seemed more nervous than normal.

"Do—uh, do you. . .want, uh, have a lot of homework?"

"No, just a little."

His lips parted, as if to say something. In those brief seconds, a minty scent escaped his mouth, making me breathless.

A few steps later, he stopped and turned to me. "Do you want to go out with me?"

In an instant, my cheeks reddened, and my feet seemed to flutter off the ground. I could have stayed in that moment forever.

"Yes," I answered, eyes smiling.

Just when I thought things couldn't get any better, he took my hand in his. My dear Rudy had set a precedent for love at the tender age of fourteen. He taught me how love was patient by waiting to be my boyfriend for two years. At home, when I did the dishes, he would stand next to me and remind me to wash the handle of the utensils, and I learned how a couple can share responsibilities. Today, he's the reason for my favorite chore.

Our most meaningful experience occurred one early evening three days later. We were sitting on my twin bed listening to '80s music on New York's WABC radio station. The door to my room was open, and Mom was in the kitchen making a typical Cuban dinner—breaded sirloin steak, fried sweet plantains, black beans and white rice—when Rudy asked, "Can I kiss you?"

*Oh, boy.* "Yes," I said nervously. I hadn't been kissed before and hoped that practicing on my hand would pay off.

He leaned over; the feeling was surreal as I floated in air. It seemed too good to be true, yet it was real, and I was ecstatic.

Rudy's loving ways melted my heart, and I had no doubt that love was kind when we treated one another with respect. My every breath seemed to revolve around him.

Our fairytale, however, did not end happily ever after. After three spectacular weeks, my heart was shattered when Rudy broke up with me for no apparent reason. I thought my world had collapsed. I did all I could at that moment to hold my well of tears inside, but when I got home, I sobbed. Emotions at thirteen are so heartfelt, and you swear you will die without your love.

To make matters worse, my prince and his family were moving to a faraway land that coming fall, but not before he said good-bye.

"I'm leaving," he said, resignation marked on his face.

All I could do was sigh; a conversation would've brought me to tears.

Then his words lifted my heavy heart. "I'll come back for you when I'm eighteen."

The hopeful child in me believed him.

Softly, he said, "Think of me when you hear 'Wishing on a Star,' and I'll think of you, too." He embraced me with tenderness, and then he left.

I cried my heart out like never before. His living in Florida was the equivalent of living on Mars. I was devastated, certain that I would never love again.

For a few years, we talked on the phone and sent each

other love letters, until life took over. Days turned into months, and I don't know when or why we lost touch, but we did. Before we knew it, we had graduated high school, and our separate futures had begun.

Throughout the years, Rudy remained on my mind, and when life became difficult or relationships soured, memories of innocent love reminded me that life still contained splendor. I thanked God for having blessed me with a once in a lifetime experience that left me wondering what would've happened if we had stayed in touch.

In 2001, I searched and found someone with his name living in Florida. The butterflies in my stomach returned as I dialed his number.

"Hello," he answered.

*It's him!* His voice had not changed. I felt like a kid all over again. "Rudy, it's me, Julia."

"Julia Torres?

"Yes."

"Wow!"

"I'll be visiting Mom and my sister, Marlene, in Florida this summer. You wanna meet?" I asked.

"Yes. That'd be great."

It was overwhelming, so much that we ended the conversation—still in disbelief that we had reconnected.

At Mom's house a few months later, I anticipated Rudy's arrival. A warm breeze stirring the leaves of palm trees, and residents watering plants were a common sight on that gorgeous afternoon, when a silver Honda Accord entered the community complex lot. *It's gotta be him.* My heart skipped a beat.

I was trying to make out the driver as the vehicle pulled

closer, but I would've recognized him anywhere.

Turning to Mom and Marlene, I shouted, "He's here!"

Rudy had climbed out of his vehicle and walked toward Mom's villa. Wearing shorts, a t-shirt, and sneakers, my dear Rudy hadn't changed much—thin build, slow and casual walk, only the hair a tad darker.

At thirty-four, I hadn't changed much either. "Rudy!" I called out, waving from the door.

Memories are incredible sensations; they seem to appear all of a sudden, and no matter how old you are, you go back in time.

"Julia." He smiled that same half smile.

There was a pause as we looked at one another in contemplation and then embraced—the memory of young love enveloping us. "Rudy!" Mom and Marlene shouted with joy as we entered. Then, of course, Mom asked, "Do you want espresso?"

The four of us sat around the cozy dining room table, slowly sipping our family staple while sharing stories of the simpler life.

Rudy and I went for a stroll afterward as birds chirped through tree-lined streets. We spoke of the mutual affection once shared that had never been duplicated, and we knew that was what had made our reunion special.

Before he left, I asked the one question that had been on my mind. "Rudy, where were you at eighteen?"

There was a pause. "I know what you're talking about," he said, "I don't know why I didn't come back. I should have."

He had remembered after all. Rudy had become the man, husband, and father that was becoming evident at fourteen, and I was proud of him. We vowed to stay in touch.

# 3

# Bulldogs

T HINGS WILL NEVER BE *the same again, but memories last forever.*
The words I wrote in my 1985 yearbook couldn't have been more accurate, nor would I have known how prophetic they'd be.

The year was 1981. Skinny jeans, leg warmers, and short skirts were the fads. Charles and Diana's wedding was the ceremony of the century, while Atari games like Pac-Man, Donkey Kong, and Centipede were all the craze. Classic performers like U2 signed with Island Records, and Bruce Springsteen released his first Top Ten hit single, "Hungry Heart."

School began on a cool, sunny morning after Labor Day. I was nervous and excited, hoping that the next four years would be filled with fun times and good friends.

Entering Ralph Waldo Emerson High School, silver-toned

metal lockers on both sides of long hallways, and decorated bulletin boards affirmed the exhilarating moment: I was an Emerson Bulldog.

Through the double doors of the vast study hall, I paused at the entrance and looked for an empty chair as hundreds of eager ninth-graders sat around long tables. Guys high-fived each other in greeting, and girls squealed with delight at the sight of old friends. Just when I thought there'd be no one familiar, I saw Lola's cheerful face.

Dolores Guerrero was her given name, but it was nowhere near as much fun as her nickname. We'd known one another in Edison, but she had kept to herself. Her bright smile and expressive almond-shaped eyes lit up the room further when she called out. "Hey, Jules! Sit here!"

Making my way down the ramp, I waved with excitement. Removing my dark blue canvas JanSport backpack, I pulled out one of the few empty chairs.

"How was your summer?" she asked.

"Great, but too short like always. Yours?"

"Really good. Did you try out for cheerleading?"

"No, my confirmation practices were at the same time, and my mom wouldn't let me miss 'em. You know how that goes," I replied in resignation.

"Yeah, I know. . .what a bummer." Lola had blossomed into a social butterfly and now talked as much as I did.

"Hey Lola, you wanna join the track team with me?"

"Sure!" We weren't exceptional runners, and Lola was better than me, but it enabled my Garifuna friend and I to become closer.

"Okay, freshmen, listen up," a strong voice shouted. "I'm

Mr. Coccioli, your class advisor. You should all have the schedules mailed to you over the summer. When you hear your name and homeroom, please line up with your designated teacher." Lola and I separated and agreed to meet for our seventh period lunch.

High school moved fast; it seemed to be all about timing. Rushing from class to class, up and down the stairs, through the annex bridge to the gym, it was exhausting, but the added responsibility made me feel happy; I was growing up!

During ninth-period Spanish, I was surprised to see my Edison friend, Mandy. We had met in kindergarten, but at the end of fifth grade we'd lost touch when she relocated.

Between whispers, Mandy and I exchanged numbers. By the end of that night's conversation, our friendship had resumed where it had left off.

I did not have any classes with Miguel throughout high school, and Bruno and Jesus moved away. Although the four of us drifted apart, today we remain friends.

When the dismissal bell rang, I met my siblings, Marlene and Frank, outside.

My sister was a senior, but besides our walks to and from school, I seldom saw her during the day. Shy and cautious, she was the teen you'd least suspect of being at fault when there was trouble. My outspoken and daring nature often caused friction between us, especially when we expected each to behave like the other, but as we grew older, we learned to accept one another's differences.

ROMANTIC AT HEART LIKE MOM, she enjoyed curling up in bed on a Friday night and reading a Harlequin romance novel or some 19<sup>th</sup>-century love story. Her goals were to become an interior designer, move to Florida, and open up her own show-room, precisely what she accomplished after college.

We shared a love for art, education, and travel, which we considered to be an adventure. Her artistic talents remain with me today when I decorate, remembering her comment, "Accessories make the home!"

Frank was a sociable, business-minded junior. His hard work led him to own a car and a motorcycle by his senior year. At twenty-one, he started his own real estate business.

He was often compared to actors like Henry Winkler, who played Fonzie in the sitcom *Happy Days*, Sylvester Stallone, and Andy Garcia, which he took great pleasure in because of their good looks and cool status. He did not participate in any sports during high school because it would have prevented him from making money; however, he was in Emerson's Modeling Club, which I joined to model with him his final two years.

With a knack for knowing the name of a song after hearing a few notes, it was no surprise that he became one of the disc jockeys in our high school. Today, he still DJs on occasion. From him, I learned a lot about music and cars—two things I am fond of.

The Torres household never lacked leadership or good work ethics, the latter of which Mom taught us by working long hours at a factory. Her struggles showed us to get an education or learn a lucrative trade.

On a negative note, we fought often and held grudges as a result of our stubborn nature. Mom, who was not one to provide firm discipline, wouldn't get involved. Eventually we'd speak without offering apologies. Having a father whose boundaries we'd respect might have made a difference in our lives.

Ambling down the hallway at school the next day, I bumped into Cecille, a Filipino student and fellow Edison cheerleader who'd been Tricia's best friend. Since she attended a different school, Cecille and I became buddies.

"Hey, chic, are you trying out for next year's cheer team?" she asked near my locker.

"Yeah, you?"

"Yup."

When the list of those who had made it was posted, we were ecstatic to see our names.

Cecille and I enjoyed cheering at Emerson's basketball games, but it was the football games at Roosevelt Stadium in Union City that were the highlights. The traditional "Turkey Game" played between Emerson and our in-district rival, Union Hill High School, occurred every year on Thanksgiving. Current and past alumni from both schools looked forward to it, which ultimately served as a high-spirited reunion.

The next four years kept me busy as I participated in an assortment of activities: school clubs, working part-time, partying in New York City at Studio 54 and Xenon, and furthering my interest in photography. High school would contain the typical teenage experiences, involving one or all four of my best friends, Mandy, Lola, Cecille, and Marissa, who'd join us our sophomore year.

Before we knew it, freshman year ended, and we were officially sophomores. That year presented a major challenge— the realization that death is indiscriminate. For the first time in our lives, Lola and I attended a wake.

In quiet dread, we entered the funeral home, glancing at classmates—some talking, others silent. The scene seemed illusory, until we noticed the black felt board with white-tacked letters: *Jose Rodriguez.*

Our friend's death had been senseless: an allergic reaction to a medication at the hospital. It was hard to believe that Jose, known as Butch, a sixteen-year-old quick with a joke, was gone. In the coffin, Butch lay stiff, zest for life no longer visible. Stunned, we turned to find a seat, noticing two chairs in the rear of the room.

Once there, Lola's nerves got the best of her, and she started to giggle. Knowing it would be contagious, I realized that as normal as it was, it was better to leave.

OUR WALK HOME IN THE MODERATE TRAFFIC was silent. Knowing that death could come to anyone at any time was a harsh reality, too cruel to accept—as in the movie *Stand By Me*, when the child actors in search of the dead body of a missing boy their own age, discovered his lifeless corpse.

We shuffled home with heavy hearts, minds amiss, oblivious to the occasional sounds of blaring horns and screeching police sirens. There was no question that the impact of Butch's early death matured us. For me however, it set the foundation for an extremely painful death the following year.

# 4

# From Blues to Hues

NOTHING PREPARED ME FOR THE TWO cataclysmic events that occurred my junior year, broke my heart, and changed my life.

One bright afternoon in front of school, I was talking to my cute, flirty friend, Eddie. His personality can be described by the American television series *Cheers'* theme song, "Where Everybody Knows Your Name," due to his fun-loving attitude and non-judgmental ways.

During our chat, my eyes caught a glimpse of sophomore Noah Otero, the football player I had been admiring in secret. Not being one who missed much, Eddie raised his eyebrows.

"Who are you looking at Miss Julia?"

"That guy. . .the one with the books in his hand." I signaled with my chin.

"Oh, Mr. Noah," he eagerly affirmed.

"You know him?"

"But of course. He's my best friend's brother."

"Does he have a girlfriend?" I asked nervously.

"No. Why, do you like him?"

"Yeah, I think he's cute."

Eddie relayed the message without my knowledge.

About a week later after school, amid classmates' chatter and boisterous laughter, Mandy and I were enjoying the cool breeze when Noah suddenly appeared in front of me. Everything around me became silent; I wondered if he could hear the loud beating of my heart.

Standing at 5'9", with hair so dark it shone, he studied me through dark eyes. His Ivory-soap-and-mothballs fresh scent enveloped me. "I heard you like me. Is that true?"

*What kind of question's that?* Help! I glanced at Mandy, but she was no longer there. *Where'd she go?* "Yes," I replied.

"Can I have your number?" he asked.

Hoping my nerves wouldn't betray me, I repeated the number in my head before relaying it.

"Okay, I'll call you tonight." As quickly as he had approached me, he left.

*What just happened?* I wanted to shout in glee, but instead I kept calm and looked around for Mandy. When I found her, I relayed everything before hurrying home.

That evening, I jumped every time the phone rang. Once again, I twirled the yellow telephone cord between my fingers. "Hello?"

"Julia?"

*It's him.* "Yeah," I answered coolly.

"It's me, Noah. What's up?" A relationship with the boy

who would be my high school sweetheart began with that phone call.

He visited the house often, and Mom always invited him for dinner, finding him a well-mannered, respectful young man. Everything in my life was wonderful—until something dreadful happened.

Abuela, my favorite family member, was admitted to the hospital in early January 1984 after complaining of severe pain. Her diagnosis, cancer of the liver, was something I did not want to believe.

During hospital visits, scenes of our family's journey from Cuba to the United States played in my head. In the much-cherished movie, Abuela was the star.

Born on April 3, 1920, in Guines, Cuba, and named Engracia Gloria Ramirez Gutierrez, Abuela was nicknamed *Felicidades* (happiness) for her zest of life. It was a word she often used when she heard negative conversation; I wish she'd said it then.

She was my jolly giant, not so much in stature but in appeal. I loved spending weekends in her cozy apartment, where she'd bring *café con leche* on a tray with buttered bread or crackers as she hummed.

A woman ahead of her time, she was the person in my family who understood me most. Abuela would've supported my career choices rather than stick with old-fashioned stereotypes about women's roles in society.

In Cuba, she had fallen in love with Celio Fundora Rosales, a handsome, dashing Cuban soldier and police officer. They'd had two children, Mom (Gloria Daisy) and my uncle, Exiquo Ramon.

The elder of the two by one year, Mom was an intelligent, happy child. Her future would have been brighter had my grandparents not divorced when Mom was eight years old, compelling her to mature earlier than her peers.

Exuding the patience and quiet strength I admire in men, Tio was my father figure. His foresight to see what would follow when President Fulgencio Batista was ousted from his position by Fidel Castro's July 26th movement led Tio to move to Mexico. Soon enough, Fidel declared himself a Marxist-Leninist, and Cuba ultimately became a full-scale Communist country.

In 1966, Tio illegally crossed the Mexican border into the United States with the intention of getting us out of Cuba, as well as living in the land of freedom and opportunity. He requested political asylum, a process made possible by John F. Kennedy's open-door policy, and later filed a petition on our behalf.

Mom could not wait for it to be approved; in the interim, she had to work exhausting hours in coffee and sugar cane fields for two years without pay, as a penalty for planning to leave the island.

On April 17, 1970, we arrived in America. My parents, who had already divorced in Cuba, parted ways. My dad went to live with his brother in California, and we went to New Jersey, where Tio helped us assimilate to our new life.

THE LOVELY FOOTAGE STOPPED when Abuela's eyes turned yellow. It became static. Although her condition had worsened, true to her nickname even on her deathbed, she remained happy.

One wintry February 16, 1984, I went home for lunch from school. The sunlight was pouring through the kitchen window, making the pale yellow paint brighter when I unlocked the door of our second-floor apartment. I was thinking how cheerful it looked for mid-February, until I saw Mom. Everything turned bleak. I knew the inevitable had occurred.

She was standing in front of the refrigerator placing a plastic pitcher of water inside. Her face was anguished—jaw clenched, deep lines on her forehead, eyes tired, lips tight. Hearing me enter, she turned. "Your grandmother died."

My world stilled, and the news cut through my heart.

"I'm going back to school," I said, gripping the keys harder.

Lunch forgotten, the reality of Abuela's death engulfed my mind as I walked somberly down the stairs, causing every step to creak. The rough wooden handrail I seldom used now served as my crutch.

I paused to look at the row of mailboxes in the entryway, each with a bell beneath, reminding me of who I was and where I lived—*Torres, 2R.* Maybe if I press it, I thought, the buzz would zap Abuela back to life.

I lumbered outside, around the corner, and up the long block. Seeing how shrubbery and trees could have life, but not Abuela, I found the world unjust.

Every house looked as old and drab as the next. Barking dogs, and honking car horns, intruded on the beautiful thoughts I wanted to keep untainted in my mind.

Little did I realize how essential her presence would have been in my future, and how lamentable it was that she had died before I found myself in an abyss too deep to climb out of for a long time.

Lola was the first friendly face I saw at school. Her smile faded when she noticed me heading to the bathroom. "You okay?" she asked, opening the heavy door.

Turning to her, I said, "No. My grandmother died."

We cried together until the bell rang. I had shuffled down the hallway and up the stairs, trying to keep up with other students, Lola on my trail, when I saw Noah. He stepped out of his descending line, gently took me out of mine and hugged me. The intensity of his embrace sheltered my grief. That was the Noah I loved.

For the next three nights, we walked to the funeral home after cheerleading and football practices, where we remained until Mom drove us home. On the fourth day, Abuela was buried.

Time continued, and so did my relationship with Noah. I met his family, including his stepbrother, Teddy, who later dated my sister. Having similar dispositions, we became good friends. Today, we share a brother-sister love that neither time nor distance has changed, but as ideal as it might have been back then, neither relationship was meant to endure. A while later, Teddy and Marlene broke up, and not too long after, Noah broke my heart.

One evening after dinner, we'd been watching television in the living room. The ticking of the clock was loud, so much that we'd wrap it in a towel, put it inside the bathroom, and close the door.

Mom was in her bedroom, getting her clothes ready for work the next day, and checked in on us from time to time.

Without preface, he began, "We've been going out like six

months now. . . ."

Turning to face him, I said, "Yeah?"

"And, um. . .we're still somewhere on second base."

"Um-hm." I don't like where this is going, I thought.

". . .And my friends have all hit home-runs."

"And?" I knew what he was alluding to, but he was un-comfortable bringing it up, and I didn't want to make it any easier for him. I was a virgin at seventeen. My definition of fun in high school had not included sex.

"Well, um, you know. . . ."

"What?"

"Well, they've been with their girlfriends less time than us, and. . . ."

"And what?"

"And, um. . .we can't hit a home run if we don't cover all the bases."

I wished he'd just been direct. "Are you trying to say that if we don't have sex, we're breaking up?"

He paused, and I knew his answer. . .it hurt. "Yes."

"I guess we're breaking up then. Nobody gives me an ul-timatum."

He said nothing but rose, heading toward the door. I opened it. The door closed on what I had deemed a blissful relationship. I wept. Mom's advice regarding break-ups came to mind: "Relationships are like bus stops. If one doesn't work out, you can hop off and get on the next one."

Although sex had never been openly discussed with us girls, she'd made one thing clear: "If you girls come home pregnant, you will have the baby. There will be no abortions in this house." Mentioning pregnancy did not mean she gave us permission to have sex. Marlene and I were to remain virgins until we were married. Frank was the only one who received the sex talk.

My mother had worked very hard to ensure we had what we needed, I couldn't hurt her by betraying her trust. Although I'd made the right decision, I'd question it in the years to follow.

The school year had come to a close and work turned fulltime that uneventful summer. Before I knew it, September had arrived.

The best football game of our four years occurred at our senior year Turkey Game. While cheering, a sudden surge of excitement took over the crowd. The band music stopped and so did we. We turned to face the field and watched an incredible sight: George Marin, Number 23, a tight-end senior player, had caught the quarterback's interception pass and was running for the touchdown from the four-yard line at lightning speed. The crowd went wild! That play had earned George the MVP award, and gave us students boasting rights.

College applications had been sent out that October. Since I'd be paying for my education through financial aid and student loans, I had to remain local; I submitted my portfolio to Rutgers University's Mason Gross School of the Arts, and waited.

In the Spring, I tore open the response envelope and shouted! Things were moving along. The end of the school year was approaching and seniors were preparing for the prom, but I hadn't given much thought to a date.

Sometime that year, a shared interest in photography had started a friendship between Judas, a fellow senior and student council member, and me. When Mandy, Cecille, and I were returning on the school bus from our club's trip, he asked me to go to the prom with him. I agreed to go as friends.

A few weeks later at the corner store after school, Marissa shared some interesting news. "I know someone who likes you."

"Is he tall, dark and handsome?" I joked.

"Um. . .yeah."

"Who?" I asked.

"George Marin."

George was the kind of the guy that guys liked to hang out with and girls found cute. His looks were often compared to those of actor Richard Gere. I was flattered.

"You wanna go on a double date to the carnival this week-end with me and Jack?" Marissa asked.

Jack was her boyfriend and George's best friend. "Sure."

On Saturday night, the four of us walked to the grounds of the St. Michael's Monastery in lively conversation.

"Let's go on the Ferris wheel," shouted Jack over carnival music.

George handed the tickets to the attendant, and I warned, "Whatever you do, don't rock it."

It stopped at the very top, and he smiled mischievously. I grabbed the metal bar and screamed.

When the ride ended, I ran out of that seat as fast as I could, hoping not to puke my guts out. "You know that wasn't funny, right?" I said to George.

"Really!" He laughed, but I couldn't be mad at him. He had an incredible smile that brightened any moment.

After walking around aimlessly, Jack and Marissa led the

way back to her house.

"You goin' to the prom?" I asked George.

"Nah. I'm not interested."

"Oh, like Jack."

"Yeah. You going?"

"Yeah, with Judas, but just as friends."

"That's cool. . .I'm going to the Marine Corps after graduation."

"Oh, wow."

"How 'bout you? Where you goin'?" he asked.

"Rutgers."

"Cool," he answered. "Wanna keep in touch while I'm in the Corps? I'll be on leave in October. We can start going out then," George suggested.

"Okay," I agreed.

That was the beginning of an unforgettable relationship.

# 5

# Wolf in Sheep's Clothing

ON THAT FIRST SUMMER EVENING, the sun shone through the open bedroom window as I peered out, anxiously waiting for my prom night to begin. While a mother strolled with her toddler down the block toward the Cuba Bakery, neighborhood men gathered outside the corner bodega near the assorted fruit and vegetable stand, sharing animated stories and whistling at pretty women.

Like the birds flying overhead, I soared, reminiscing on my last four years. High school had been everything I'd imagined it would be, and there was no doubt in my mind that life would get better.

At last, the big shiny white limo pulled up amid the bustle of traffic, double-parking in front of my six-family apartment building. Judas rang the bell and came up to greet me, looking handsome in his pressed black tuxedo. Mandy and her date,

Anthony, were waiting downstairs.

Holding a clear plastic rectangular box containing a white rose corsage, he raised his brows, smiled and said, "You look nice. Here, this is for you."

"You, too. Thanks. I'll put it on my shawl." My ivory dress, the lower half silk, the upper half strapless lace, couldn't hold a corsage. "I have something for you, too." I carefully fastened a boutonnière on his lapel, its scent wafting through the air. "There you go."

"Thank you. You ready?"

"Yeah, but my mom wants to take some pictures first." We held our smiles, overlooking the bright flash at the snap of each photograph.

Thinking back, the onset of the blaring light freezes that point in time. It would be the critical moment when my life, as simple as it was, changed forever. Maybe if Mom had an inkling of what would happen, she would've warned me; instead, I kissed her good-bye and walked out the door with a big innocent smile and bright blissful eyes. As she excitedly called out to have fun, I turned to wave and caught a glimpse of her proud, tear-filled eyes.

Stepping into the limo and seeing Mandy and Anthony dressed to impress made the evening a reality! "Mandy, you look great!" Looking particularly regal in a royal blue dress that complemented her porcelain skin, dark brown hair, and hazel eyes, Mandy looked older in her high heels, elegant hairstyle, and make-up.

"You too, Julia! Sit here," she said, moving her satin clutch to the side and patting the comfortable leather seat beside her.

I turned to Anthony, dressed similarly to Judas, who sat across from her. "You look nice. Your bud is a perfect match for her dress."

"Yeah, it is. Thanks. So do you."

Mandy and I began talking in the enthusiastic way teenage girls tend to, and Anthony and Judas began their own conversation. When we pulled into the vast entrance of the Westmount Country Club in West Paterson, New Jersey, some classmates were exiting blue, gold, and black limos, as others strolled in jubilant conversation toward the entrance.

The palette of dresses ranged from ivory white and pastels to earth tones and sophisticated black, ideal combinations for the varying hairstyles and make-up. The guys looked handsome in their tuxedos or suits, each distinguished by the color of his cummerbund, bow tie, or carnation on his lapel. It was nice to see their strong, curious faces, suggesting the young men they were becoming.

Leaving the limo's plush interior, forgetting the casual footsteps of Judas and Anthony behind us, our heels clicked on the driveway pavers, every step faster than the next. Floral and leafy fragrances surrounded us as we joined the cacophony of high-pitched laughter and optimistic baritone greetings befitting our moods—powerful, energetic, and fascinating.

Marveling at the beauty of our first impression, we paused to take in the lobby's grandeur—a softly lit, elaborate chandelier creating a kaleidoscope of rich hues of red, green, and burgundy.

The DJ's loud disco and free-style music increased the exuberant voices as Mandy and I rushed to open a set of white doors with gold handles leading to the grand ballroom. Inside, the marble dance floor was large enough to hold a sea of people; tables decorated in our blue-and-white school colors accentuated the Bulldog pride we felt.

From afar, we spotted Lola and Cecille standing by our table and waved with exaggerated glee. Lola's silk mustard gown was ideal against her smooth chocolate skin. Exuding a fun, fervent teenager and a poised young lady, her bobbed hairstyle warmly shaped her oval face.

Cecille's voluminous hair and knowing eyes were stunning—a pristine fit for her dress. The gold fabric draped her curves magically and brought a pink hue to her cheeks. Yes indeed, we were all blossoming into lovely young women.

Chatter and loud laughter began the minute we approached the table. Before you knew it, the four of us were on the dance floor. We felt as if the evening revolved solely around us.

There is much to be said of old friends: No matter what you are doing, you always have a great time. High school is when the friendships you make seem to matter the most.

Judas was a perfect gentleman throughout the evening, leaving me alone to enjoy the time with the girls, while he spent time with his friends. As a group, the only time we were together was to eat and have the table picture taken.

When ravenous appetites were appeased with scrumptious chicken and pasta in Alfredo sauce, or a savory steak and a bountiful baked potato, soda and water quenched our thirst. But when the dessert arrived, we knew the night would soon end. We ate as fast as we could, and dashed onto the dance floor for the last songs.

"Man, I can't believe tonight's almost over!" shouted

Mandy in disbelief, while clapping to the electrifying beat.

"I know. I wish it'd never end," I added.

"Me, too," said Cecille, placing her head on my shoulder.

"I'm gonna miss you guys!" cried Lola, cupping her delicate hands together. "Ain't no mountain high enough!" she yelled.

Lola had predicted the last song. "Ain't No Mountain High Enough," by Diana Ross, was usually one of two songs that played at the end of our high school dances; the other being "Last Dance" by Donna Summer. We began to sing, swaying with our arms around each other as tears flowed, hugs intensified, and kisses were graciously given. Before we could stop the clock from ticking, prom night had ended with as much splendor as it had begun. High school was now in our past. Friends would part, and a new phase of life would soon begin.

The thrill remained as Mandy, Anthony, Judas, and I entered our limo and asked the driver to take us to Manhattan, where we entered a nightclub. Although it was fun, it lacked the excitement of our prom. We eventually agreed to head back to Jersey to grab a bite at the Coach House Diner in North Bergen.

It was one of two places that teenagers from the surrounding towns of West New York and Union City frequented after clubbing in Manhattan. The other was White Castle, a fast-food burger place across from James Braddock Park, known to locals as 80th Street Park.

We stood in the busy foyer waiting to be seated. The aroma of coffee, bacon, and eggs reminded our growling stomachs how famished we were. Across from us, a tall glass counter displayed a wide selection of decadent desserts—delicious pies and mouth-watering cakes. But the lights seemed too bright after dancing in dim light, and the chatter of strangers appeared to crowd the high of our special night.

"Hello. How many will you be?" the host asked.

"Four," we replied in unison.

She grabbed some menus near the old cash register. "Right this way. You guys all look great!"

"Thank you. We just had our prom," Mandy beamed with pride.

"Oh, how exciting!"

"Yeah, it was great!" I added.

She smiled and, after reaching our table, said, "Well, have a seat. Your server will be with you shortly."

Each of us ordered deluxe cheeseburgers, meaty and cooked just right; the fries, a lovely golden color, seemed to come out of an advertisement. Even the Pepsi Cola tasted perfect; its first gulp bringing out a refreshing sigh.

"So what'd you guys think about the prom?" I asked between burger bites.

"I thought it was great," answered Mandy while sipping her soda. "The music, the food. . .everybody looked really good, even the teachers. It couldn't have been better."

"Yeah, you're right," agreed Judas.

"I can't believe high school's over. Those four years flew. They were so much fun," I sighed.

Anthony turned to Mandy. "So what do we do next?"

"I dunno," she answered. "What can we do?" she asked the group, wanting to keep the euphoria's momentum.

"How 'bout we go to Seaside?" Judas suggested.

"How are we gonna get there?" I asked.

"We still have money left over. We can tell the driver to take us to our houses to get clothes, and he can drop us off," he replied.

After agreeing, we paid the bill, did as planned, and slept on the one-and-a-half-hour drive south to Seaside Heights, a resort beach community with an amusement-oriented boardwalk.

The driver tapped on the privacy glass, before bringing it down. "Good morning. You're here."

Rolling down the windows on both sides, we were met by the muggy weather and misty salt. It was already daylight when Mandy and I peered out, squinting, wondering where we'd stay. A white rectangular sign picturing a sun on the first motel we saw read Island Sun Inn. It would have to do.

We paid the driver, watched him pull away and headed to the registration office. The door was locked, so we peeked through the window for the check-in time and nightly rate. Mandy confirmed what no one wanted to hear: "Check-in's at two and it's forty bucks."

"Maybe we can get in earlier," I suggested.

"Yeah. When does it open?" Judas asked.

Mandy looked at the door's "will return" sign before saying, "Eight."

On the neat wooden counter rested a bell, behind it, a black-and-white analog clock read 6:45. "We still have a little more than an hour. Do we have enough money?" she added.

We sat on the stairwell steps and pooled our cash—fifty dollars. It wasn't enough for food and a room.

"I just got a Master Card last month," I offered. "I bought

it in case we needed it. We can charge it on my card, and you guys can pay me later."

"Phew! Good idea, Julia," said Mandy. The guys agreed.

Having resolved our place to stay, Mandy and I talked on the steps, while Judas and Anthony went to hang out on the boardwalk.

Later at the motel office, the clerk allowed us an early check-in and gave us our key.

Walking up the steps to the second story, we neared one of the blue doors on the left. To its right, sat a window air-conditioning unit. Through the drawn tan curtains, was a neat wood-paneled room.

The interior was standard: two full-sized beds with a floral comforter, a nightstand in between with a beige lamp and matching lampshade, a telephone, and a small, brown-and-black digital alarm clock. In front of the beds, below a vertical gilt mirror, ran a long, wooden dresser with two drawers on each side, and on it, a tube television, and table lamp. The only novelty was a kitchenette area to the left of the entrance, a refrigerator, table and four chairs.

"We're gonna get some beer," said Judas.

Mandy and I didn't object. We had attended house parties where we'd drink with friends and thought nothing of it. Things had never gotten out of hand. In fact, if someone drank too much, we'd speak to an adult to ensure the friend was taken home safely.

After placing our overnight bags on the bed closest to the bathroom, we took turns showering. I changed into a white crew neck t-shirt, tucked inside pink nylon Adidas running shorts, and Reebok sneakers.

When the guys returned with a case of Budweiser and drinking cups, Mandy and I went for a stroll on the boardwalk, while they took their showers. Salt water and coconut tanning oil scents reminded us we were down the shore, but unable to pay to go on the beach.

We sat on one of the whitewashed boardwalk benches to enjoy the roaring waves that crashed onto the shoreline as seagulls cried overhead. Sun worshipers sprawled out on colorful towels, while neighbors sat on lounge chairs beneath striped umbrellas sipping drinks from their coolers. No matter how carefully people walked, their steps would kick sand on someone.

It was a given; New Jersey, with its limited summer season, never fails to bring a large crowd of beachgoers from the time the shore opens on Memorial Day until it closes on Labor Day.

Hot chili dogs, charcoal-grilled burgers, and hand-tossed pizza, made my mouth water. "Mandy, you smell that?"

"Yeah. It's making me hungry."

"I'm starving. Let's go back. Maybe they're done, and we can go eat."

When we got there, the four of us left and found a burger place nearby. Again, I put the bill on my card.

Having nothing to do, we walked around aimlessly until we decided to return to the room, where we sat around the table to play quarters.

Before you knew it, Mandy had a buzz; she was missing more than me.

"I'll drink half your drink so you can keep playing," I suggested.

At some point between her halves and my drinks, I said, "Okay, I'm done. That's it for me." I rose from my chair.

"Me, too," added Mandy.

"I gotta go to the bathroom," I said.

Noticing my unsteady steps, Judas extended his left forearm. "Want some help?"

"Yeah, thanks." He escorted me to the bathroom, and I glanced at the clock: 9:00 p.m. Judas waited outside the door. When I exited, he walked me to the bed Mandy and I had claimed as ours. I lay down—alone. Immediately, I was out cold.

# 6

# Demons To Bind

IN THE MIDDLE OF THE NIGHT, I opened my eyes sluggishly and saw the shadow of Judas' face lit by the sliver of light cast through the window. His body was moving in a prone position over mine. Although I wasn't feeling anything, I realized what was happening—he was having sex with me. I had no strength, and my reflexes were extremely poor.

Struggling to speak as I tried to move my heavy head slowly, I whispered in a dazed tone, "G-get o-*off* me." On my left, the red lights of the digital alarm clock read: 12:00 a.m. *When did it start?*

"Wait," he said.

I couldn't scream. I couldn't scratch. I couldn't lift a finger.

I repeated it. This time, he listened.

My eyes followed him as he walked out the door. Then I

was out cold again.

When I awoke later that morning, I was not hung over. My mind was clear. I had no headache or cotton mouth.

The bed to my left was empty and unmade. Mandy was sleeping to the right of me, snoring lightly. The reality of what had happened was in the back of my mind, but I did not want to acknowledge it.

Removing the comforter, I rose quietly from the bed, careful not to wake her. That was when I noticed my clothing—although my shorts were the same, my t-shirt was not. It was green. *Who put this on me?* I didn't ask. I didn't want to know the details.

As I headed to the shower, I saw my white t-shirt crumpled on the floor. Near it was my yellow bikini. It was bloodstained.

At that moment, my defense mechanism began to shut me down. Stoically, I picked up my underwear and t-shirt. The stain was a grim reminder of what that sick boy had yanked from me—my virginity. In a trance, I grabbed my black nylon duffel bag and entered the bathroom.

I slid both items into my bag, took out a fresh set of clothes and showered—beating water drops a momentary solace. When I stepped out of the bathroom, Mandy was preparing her clothes for the shower. "It's all yours," I called out.

Judas had returned and was arranging his bag for checkout. Although I hadn't been awake for most of my rape, those brief seconds of incomprehensible images replayed in my mind. Perhaps it would've been better if I hadn't awakened. Maybe ignorance would have made my life easier—but there must've been a reason for my awareness.

Placing the bag on my bed, I asked, "You guys went to the beach?"

He looked up, unsure of what to say, a t-shirt in his hand. "Yeah?"

"Was it packed?"

"Uh, yeah." He zipped up his bag.

"Where's Anthony?"

"He saw someone he knew and stayed hanging out."

"So why didn't you stay?" I walked towards him.

"I had to get this done."

By that time, I was standing to his left. "How 'bout Anthony?"

"He said he'll do it when he gets back." He seemed relieved to be speaking to me in generalities, though his eyes were shifting.

"Oh." I leaned forward and kissed him.

To make matters worse, I asked, "How was it last night?"

"Good!" he replied, nervous smirk on his face—coward, cynic, whatever he was.

His response added to my confusion. I remained silent, staring blankly at him.

The whole incident had been repulsive, its aftermath excruciating. Why had I kissed him and asked such a question? I doubted my sanity for many years.

The sound of the bathroom door opening broke my spell. I turned to it. "Mandy, you wanna go with me to call my brother so he can pick us up?"

When we returned, Judas and Anthony were sitting on the bed, watching television. "My brother's picking us up. We're checking out now," I said.

Mandy and I grabbed our bags. So did they.

I glanced at the open case of beer on the floor before leaving. It underscored what had happened, the red and white colors a stale mockery. Some cans were in the garbage, others unopened. What would the walls say if they could speak? We hadn't finished all the beer, yet I hadn't asked myself why I had felt numb, immobile, as if I'd been drugged.

The door closed abruptly behind us, and with it went my peace. The hardship I'd have to endure to reclaim it would take a very long time.

After Mandy and I left the key with the clerk, we sat on the steps to wait for Frank. The guys stood near the window of the motel office. About thirty minutes later, a green Chevy Impala pulled up; I recognized my mom's friend, Viton, behind the wheel. My brother was beside him.

They approached us on the stairs. "You ready?" Frank asked.

"Yeah. The guys are over there."

"I'm not taking those fuckin' guys. Let 'em find their own fuckin' ride."

I was glad my brother decided not to bring them. I couldn't have imagined being cramped in the back seat with Judas.

Bags between us, the four doors shut at different times, each with more of a thud. No one looked back.

Mindlessly, I stared out the window at the cars on the turnpike, allowing Frank's mixed cassette tape to cloud my thoughts but paying no attention to the music I loved.

From what seemed afar, I heard Mandy whisper, "Julia?"

"What?"

"Look what I found near Judas' bag." She had a crinkled piece of aluminum foil in her right palm.

"When'd you find it?"

"This morning when I was getting my stuff ready. You were in the shower."

"Did you open it?"

"No, I was waiting for you."

"Oh, go ahead."

She unfolded the foil until it lay flat. There was a residue of white powder on it.

"Cocaine?" she asked.

"Yeah," I said. "I didn't know he did drugs."

"Me neither."

Shrugging, I returned my gaze to the window, not caring why she had told me. I wanted to eradicate the whole thing from my mind. Saying it had happened would make it real, then I'd have to confront it. I wasn't prepared to.

Viton stopped in front of Mandy's house. She paused outside, bag in hand. "Good-bye, Julia."

I looked through her. "Bye."

Mandy went up the steps without turning. I only saw my kindergarten friend once after that night. We never discussed what happened. Our childhood friendship had been irretrievably shattered. Whoever thinks rape solely affects the victim is grossly mistaken.

A clean smell of bleach welcomed me when I entered my apartment. Mom was listening to music while doing laundry in the kitchen. On the patterned linoleum floor, piles of whites, darks, and colors were ready to be thrown in the washing machine.

*Oh, good.* I unzipped my bag and removed my prom dress and dirty clothes but left the unsettling bikini inside.

"How was the prom?" she asked, tossing in the whites.

"Good. Here's the dress for the cleaners, Ma. You can give it away. You should've seen how great the girls looked."

I threw in my dirty whites, making sure the water covered the t-shirt by pushing it down further. If only the bleach could've made me as whole as I had been.

"Did you take lots of pictures?"

"Pretty much." I tossed my pink shorts and green shirt in their piles and involuntarily brushed my hands together.

"Where'd you go after?" she asked, pulling out the knob to start the washing machine.

The sound of water has always been therapeutic for me— rain, a waterfall, a tap. It was no different when the cycle began. "We went to a club in New York, ate at the Coach House, and then went down the shore."

"You had fun?"

"Ma, I'm tired. I'm gonna take a nap."

I said nothing else. I hid the bikini in a corner of my undergarment drawer and fell asleep.

I hadn't told her about my rape because I knew she would not have been supportive. Had I felt otherwise, I would have, and maybe she could've guided me, but in her eyes I would've been the culprit and I didn't know what I would've done if my own mother had blamed me.

Also, I figured that Frank's response would've been predictable—to beat the crap out of him. I would've appreciated it at the time, but it would not have been the unconditional acceptance I needed to help me heal. I sensed that he would've blamed me for having placed myself in what he deemed as a precarious position, so I couldn't tell him either.

I kept the truth from Marlene, who was righteous and somewhat more open-minded, but even the slightest negative perception from her would've crushed me mentally and emotionally. I didn't want to take the chance.

This left me to carry that beast of burden on my narrow shoulders, dispirited and alone. My ability to trust, maybe even more destructively than my virginity, had been destroyed. I began creating walls of self-preservation. No one would get through unless I let them.

Initially, I didn't know what to think. I felt as if I were living in a daze. I was in such a state of confusion. My entire life seemed surreal. I tried to tell myself I'd had sex with a friend, but knew I couldn't have, since I had been unconscious, and the two did not equate. For a while, I kept the underwear. The darkened bloodstain was the only material evidence of what I had lost. It would become the prelude to the dark ground I'd trod.

A few weeks later, the prom pictures arrived. Mom put the 8x10" picture in a beautiful frame. Telling her to remove it from the living-room armoire would have created suspicion, so I maintained my silence.

Whenever I passed that photograph, I shut down further. After a while, I got so good at it that I began to see through the picture, and it no longer affected me. Seemingly as time passed, I started to do the same with people.

In July, I waited for my period to arrive, but it did not. I wondered what else could possibly go wrong. If I was pregnant, I knew I wouldn't have an abortion and that led me to even greater torment. I could not link the innocence of a precious infant to such a deviant act. What fault would a child have who was born that way?

I could not make matters worse by taking a life, when mine had already been taken. My head spun for the entire month as I hoped and prayed for my period.

Of all the milestones Marissa and I shared, the harshest one occurred during the first week of August—a traumatic event that altered our lives and that we have spoken of only twice.

One airy afternoon while hanging out in her bedroom with the windows open, talking about nothing in particular, her mom busied herself with household chores in the kitchen. Marissa's soothing voice contrasted sharply with the demons that gnawed in my mind, clawing with spiky talons at my brain. I didn't know how much longer I could keep silent.

Our conversation led to the prom and unable to control myself anymore, I blurted, "I had sex with Judas after."

The color drained from her face. She rose in slow motion, covering her mouth with her hands, aghast. I saw the disbelief in her widened eyes.

"Tell me what happened," she whispered with great tenderness, knowing something was wrong. She was aware of how I valued my virginity and had admired my position not to have sex with Noah.

There, in her room surrounded by posters of teen idols and low radio music, I relayed the story.

"You didn't have sex with him," she said, sitting down. "He raped you."

She had spoken the truth I did not want to hear. I looked

blankly at her, unblinking.

"There was no way you could have had sex with him, Julia. You passed out. You didn't give your consent. He raped you."

Hearing the harshness of the word "rape" did something to my psyche. I suddenly felt the urge to use the bathroom, and in a trance-like state, I shuffled to it. When I saw the fresh red bloodstain on my underwear, I felt an indescribable relief!

Shouting, I ran down the length of her railroad apartment towards her room, leaving the delicious aroma of her mom's cooking behind. "Marissa, Marissa! Fred's here!"

Greeting me with arms wide open, knowing exactly what Fred was, I welcomed her sheltering embrace. We sobbed together for a youth lost to cruelty.

She was the first person I told, and although her response was encouraging, she'd be the last I'd tell for a long time.

For seven years after Judas raped me, I was on automatic pilot following the path I presumed was meant for me. I did not notice my surroundings, nor did I stop to think. I kept on moving, overcoming hurdles, ducking, taking cover, constantly looking forward, seldom back, rarely within. My goal was to achieve difficult feats, hoping to keep at bay the demons that hovered, waiting to devour me at the slightest moment of weakness.

I was vigilant; keeping my guard up became second nature. For a long time I continued living in that broken and disturbed state.

# 7

# Be All That You Can Be

IT WAS OFFICIAL; MY MASCOT for the next four years would be a Scarlet Knight! Mom's firm advice echoed: "Girls, you must go to college to help you prepare for life. There is much freedom in financial security. You can always take care of yourself and your family without having to depend on a man, put up with infidelity or abuse. With a factory salary, you'll always struggle like me. I don't want that for you."

Marlene, the first in our immediate family to attend college, had two more years to complete her Bachelor of Fine Arts degree in Interior Design when I began my freshman year at Rutgers.

Riding up the South Tower's cramped elevator on Livingston Campus with Mom in tow, our hands, as well as those of other students and their families, were heavily laden with clothes and food.

On the seventh floor, we passed wide-open dorm rooms blasting with music and smelling of incense. My roommate was listening to music from a small boom-box on the top shelf of her desk, her section of the room already organized.

"Hi, I'm Julia Torres," I called out.

"I'm Pat Lozano," she replied, lowering the volume, turning to Mom to offer help.

She smiled warmly at the tall, thin Ecuadorian from Bergenfield, New Jersey, delighted to hear that she spoke Spanish.

Pat and I got along splendidly. Both of us were night owls; we'd stayed up listening to music while sharing tidbits of our lives.

One late evening, as Pat stood eating her usual pint of chocolate ice cream out of the carton, she tapped the back of the tablespoon against her front teeth and said, "Julie, you were destined for greatness."

Sitting on my bed, writing a letter to George, I looked up, startled at her firm tone, but said nothing. I didn't know what had driven her to say that, but her words caused me to remember an experience I'd had in the church youth group.

Marlene, who'd had the idea of uplifting a prison inmate, had been corresponding with John Rosa. He acquainted us with the true essence of God when he suggested we visit a Pentecostal church in our area named Monte De Oracion. Mom, Marlene, and I went one Sunday afternoon, and our lives changed forever.

Accustomed to listening to a priest's sermon in silence, we sat in awe as church members praised God aloud. "Glory to God!" and "Hallelujah!" were phrases of worship heard throughout the church as the pastor preached.

My siblings and I had completed the traditional baptism, confession, and confirmation ceremonies, as well as attended catechism classes on Sundays, but we had never opened a Bible. At Monte de Oracion, when the pastor quoted or read scripture, members followed suit with their own Bibles. We read more of God's Holy Word in those two hours than we had in our entire lives.

We felt that the true meaning of God and faith had not been taught to us, especially after feeling the warm presence inside that church. It wasn't the temperature of the room or the friendly people, and we wondered what it could be attributed to, but after going more often, we understood that what we had sensed was the Holy Spirit's presence. Our knowledge of God and the Bible grew as we learned further that, before Jesus was crucified, He told his disciples that He would leave behind a Counselor (John 14:16) who'd remain on Earth on His behalf—the Holy Spirit.

We began reading the Bible together and started to comprehend the reality of God, Jesus, and the Holy Spirit. The Trinity became more personal, not mere words, just as confessing our sins with true repentance and praying in the name of Jesus, meant that God would hear our prayers and forgive us. It was that simple; no prerequisites were necessary.

Questioning my Catholic upbringing, I wondered why tradition was followed rather than Christ. When I did not find a mention of purgatory in the Bible, I wondered why I had been taught a fallacy.

Within months, Marlene and I accepted Jesus as God's Son and our Lord and Savior. To demonstrate our faith and belief, we decided to be baptized in a Bronx, New York, church named Juan 3:16.

The Pentecostal baptismal process was very different from the sprinkled water I'd formerly received. After removing my shoes and placing a white gown over my clothes, I walked down a few steps into about three feet of cool water, where a pastor in similar attire instructed me to place my hands in a prayer position, thumbs against my nostrils. "Do you believe in Jesus Christ as God's Son and your Lord and Savior?" he asked.

"Yes, I do."

"I now baptize you in the name of the Father, the Son, and the Holy Spirit," he added, before immersing me backward into the water.

The baptism ended but not its celestial effect. I felt closer to God and was filled with an extraordinary peace. Later I learned that what I had felt had been the peace Jesus said he'd leave for us in John 14:27: "Peace I leave with you, my peace I give to you."

At our new church, Marlene and I looked forward to the youth group activities, whether performing skits, going on day trips, or attending prayer nights. During the latter, Andrea Castillo, the president of our club, being touched by the Holy Spirit, began speaking in tongues, as she sometimes did in church.

The first time we'd heard it, we wondered what was happening. It sounded bizarre, even a bit scary, but it became a matter of understanding the Word of God as written in 1 Corinthians 12 regarding the variety of gifts given by the Holy Spirit as He willed for the common good, such as the working of miracles, prophecy, or distinguishing between spirits. In Andrea's case, her gifts included speaking and interpreting tongues.

Approaching every youth knelt in prayer, through the Holy Spirit's revelation she prophesied something specific, but she bypassed me. *What about me?*

Believing the messages were from God, I cried quietly. Had I been so vile at thirteen years old that He would have nothing to say to me? I wondered.

Andrea did not see or hear me cry, nor could she have known my thoughts. However, God knows everything, which explains why, being led by the Holy Spirit, she approached me, speaking in tongues, and prophesied, "Don't cry. Don't be sad. I have something for you to do, but it's not your time yet."

Since then, I have wondered when those words would come to fruition. Pat's sudden remark affirmed that God had a grander purpose for my life than my own personal interests. I thought of how college, the beginning of adult life on a smaller scale, would play into it.

During my first semester, what I anticipated most was opening my campus mailbox to find a letter from George. It made my day!

One weekend that October, while reading a magazine in my dorm room as music blared from WKTU radio, there was a knock on my open door. I glanced up and leapt with joy!

Wearing jeans, sneakers, and a red-and-yellow Parris Island Marine Corps sweatshirt, George stood grinning from ear to ear. "Surprise!" he said.

I threw myself at him, absorbing his clean, piney scent.

"What a surprise, you look great, love the hair," I said in one breath, patting the top of his head. "What are you doing here?"

Gesturing toward the elevator, he asked in a joking manner, "Want me to leave?"

I grabbed his arm. "No! I didn't mean it that way!"

"I know. . .I was just kidding. I wanted to see you."

"Yay! I'm glad you came."

"I see that. You almost knocked me down," he joked.

"You're not a weakling!" I shook my head, smiling.

"Jewels, you wanna go home?"

"Yeah! You don't have to ask me twice."

Our relationship began that jovial moment.

George always found a way to see me whenever he was on leave, until April when he'd be home for good, bringing adventure and spontaneity.

Mom found his happy and protective nature endearing. Because of that, he earned her special title: *mi niño.*

As the end of freshman year approached, I found two places for summer employment that piqued my interest. One was an advertisement for photography counselors at a camp in the Rutgers newspaper, the *Daily Targum.* The other came from a commercial with a catchy jingle: "Be all that you can be. Find your future in the Army."

Realizing that I'd get more out of life if I enlisted in the military, I researched all four branches to see which would suit me best, concluding that the army wouldn't affect my studies.

One early May afternoon, I entered the recruiting station on George Street in New Brunswick. Posters and pamphlets occupied different areas of the neat office.

A recruiter wearing a green uniform sat behind a metal desk filling out paperwork. "Hello. May I help you?" he asked as I neared his desk.

"Yes." I gave him my name. "I want to enlist in the Reserves."

His small brown eyes expressed curiosity. "Oh, okay. I'm Sergeant First Class Rollo." He extended his hand.

"Before enlisting, you have to take the Armed Services Vocational Aptitude Battery, a proficiency test that measures a candidate's knowledge in various fields and determines the field of expertise one can choose for their Military Occupational Specialty, M-O-S. In other words, your job."

"Okay. How soon can I take it? I'd like to leave this summer and be back in time for next semester."

"I'll pick you up this Saturday at 0700 hours, take you to the test site in Jersey City, and bring you home when you're done. It takes all day. Make sure you get a good night's rest. Once the results are in, I'll call you."

For the remainder of the afternoon, I remained excited, knowing that I had made a very important decision in my life.

Two weeks later, in Rollo's office, he gave me my results. "Julia, based on your scores, you can choose any MOS you'd like. You scored very well in all areas."

"Wow, that's great. I like military police."

"The MP training won't get you back in time."

"Oh. So what does?"

"You have two options, cook or truck driver."

"Well, I don't wanna be a cook. That's not for me. I'd hate to be in a hot kitchen all day. I'll be a truck driver. That's pretty cool, and not a lot of women do it, so it'll be a challenge."

"All right, but you don't have to remain a truck driver. In the fall, you can enter ROTC, which is available to college students interested in becoming an officer in the armed forces. You can choose another MOS when you graduate. For now, let me explain your six-by-two enlistment contract in the Split Option program. This summer you'll complete Basic Training, next summer your MOS. After that, you'll have annual training for two weeks every summer for the remainder of your contract. Once basic is done, you'll be assigned to a reserve unit where you will drill one weekend a month and perform your MOS. For the first six years, you'll be in the reserves. For the last two, you'll be placed in IRR, Individual Ready Reserves, which means you can be called to active duty in the event of a war."

On May 26, 1986, I signed my life over to Uncle Sam at the Military Entrance Processing Station in Newark, New Jersey, pledging to defend our constitution and the American way of life—freedom.

At home that afternoon I told Mom. "I'm going to the Army."

"*What?* Why are you doing *that?*" she asked. "I've been told that there are lots of drugs in the military."

"That's a lie!" There goes Mom again, I thought, listening to other people's baseless opinions.

"It's not worth giving your life for any country. The higher-ups don't do that. You must've inherited those desires from your grandfather and his brother."

"I don't care what anybody else does. I wanna do it. I'm leaving next month to Fort Jackson, South Carolina." She didn't dwell on the news; perhaps she thought it was a crazy idea of mine that would pass.

The realization of my enlistment struck mom on June 26, 1986, when our bell rang at 0400 hours.

"Who is it?" she asked, still groggy and alarmed that someone would visit us so early.

"The sergeant," I shouted as I buzzed him in.

While Mom shuffled in, adjusting the belt of her yellow robe, a tap on the door revealed Rollo in his dress green uniform, garrison cap in hand. "You ready?" his voice echoed through the empty hallway.

"Yes, Sergeant Rollo."

"Where are you going?" Mom asked.

"I told you. Fort Jackson."

He looked puzzled.

Matter-of-factly, I explained, "Sergeant Rollo, this is my mom. She didn't believe I enlisted."

"Oh, how do you do Mrs. Torres?" he said, extending his hand.

"Fine."

Turning to me, she asked, "When will you return?"

"End of summer. Bye."

"What about George?" she asked as I left.

"We said good-bye last night."

I followed Rollo into his government car.

At Newark Airport, he said, "Turn in your orders to the uniformed sergeant at the airport. Good luck."

I boarded the aircraft, eager and excited.

THE MINUTE I GOT OFF THE PLANE, I became nervous at the

sight of the tall, muscular sergeant. My uncertain approach must have explained why I was there. "You one of mine?" he asked in defiance, firm face, tight lips.

"Yes, Sergeant." His name tag read *Hardmeyer*.

"Got orders?"

"Yes, Sergeant," I said as I began to remove them from my hooded sweatshirt pocket.

Glaring at me, he snapped, "I haven't asked you for anything! Don't be so sure of yourself."

I didn't move. *Is this how it's gonna be?*

"Now give me your orders," he commanded.

I did.

"I'm in charge here, not you," he muttered under his breath. "Damn kids."

*Oh, great, I already started out on the wrong foot.*

"Follow me," ordered Hardmeyer. He took long strides, and I almost had to run to keep up with him.

"Get in." He signaled to a bus by the exit whose destination header read *Reception Station*.

Through the windows, I could see trainees sitting inside, brows curled up in worry, jaws tight with anxiety. Another sergeant sat behind the driver's seat, impassively looking out the window.

Not knowing if I was supposed to address him, I climbed on a bit leery, glancing briefly in his direction, but he didn't move. Good, I thought, I don't want to say the wrong thing again.

Finding an empty seat, I placed the duffel bag on my lap. No one made eye contact. When Hardmeyer entered, the door shut with a swish. The ride was quiet, as uncertainty and dread mounted further.

At our destination, the doors opened to let in more sergeants.

"*Go, go, go!*" screamed the first.

"*Everybody out!*" shouted the second.

"*Move, move, move!*" yelled the third.

Some trainees bumped into each other, wondering whose voice to listen to, until we were finally outside, standing at attention.

The scent of freshly cut grass lingered in the air as one sergeant barked, "Welcome to the United States Army. We are not your drill sergeants. We are sergeants who will process you in. Listen. There are no repeats. You will be issued uniforms, taught how to wear them, and receive your gear. You will carry your own duffel bag. If it's too heavy, too bad! Deal with it! No gentlemen here. You will learn basic marching commands, so you don't look stupid in your uniform. If you brought personal items, hand them to your drill sergeants, or they will take them from you. We are not your mothers. We won't remind you. You'll get them on your way out, whenever that is." He continued in his cut-and-dry voice. "Look at the person next to you. You may not see her again. Not all of you will make it, because not all of you are equipped to be a United States soldier. Right, face!"

We did exactly as he said. A few days later when processing was complete, we stood in uniform with our gear in formation. Within minutes, several sergeants wearing Smokey-the-Bear hats arrived. They stared at us, efforts at intimidation obvious.

"You will call me, and anyone else with a hat like mine,

'Drill Sergeant.' We are not sergeants. We are better! When you hear formation, you will stop whatever you are doing and stand at attention in platoon formation. You will not move, sneeze, cough, or do anything else until told otherwise. When a drill sergeant tells you to drop, you get into a front leaning rest position and do push-ups. You stop when you are told to. We don't want to see your butt up in the air. We don't want to see you stretching. If you can't do them, leave. If you can't do sit-ups, leave. If you can't run, march, shoot, or do anything physical, we don't want you here! Some misfits have already gone home voluntarily, crying to their mommas. Others have been told by Uncle Sam they are not fit to be soldiers. Maybe there a few of you left. If you can't take it, now is your chance to get out." He paused and looked around.

I don't know what made the warm drops of sweat dripping down my head accumulate beneath my cap—the hot beaming sun or the fear the drill sergeant's megaphone voice instilled. But I prayed that he'd finish before it stung my eyes. No one moved.

"You will go to your barracks now and meet your drill sergeants. When your name is called, run to the bus that's filling up. If you have to ask me where to go, you will drop."

In no particular order, he barked, "Penn, Silletti, Perkins, DeMogola, Montañez, Woody, Torres. . . ."

Our destination would be Tank Hill—old, two-story, barracks-style housing with no air conditioning; rather, metal floor fans stood at either end of each floor.

When we arrived, a slew of drill sergeants were standing on the ground, shoulder to shoulder. From the inside of the hot bus, their rants were clear. *Shit! I hope I can do this.*

# 8

# Tank Hill

"EVERYBODY OUT!" HOLLERED THE SERGEANT at 0500 hours when he stopped the bus in front of the barracks. We grabbed the duffel bags that stood on our laps, slinging them onto our backs.

Stepping onto the vehicle, the first drill sergeant yelled, *"Move, move, move!"*

We began moving frantically amid thuds of shuffling boots.

From the ground, another drill sergeant bellowed, *"Move with a purpose. . . !"*

With every shout sounding angrier than the next, the chaos worsened. *"Go, go, go!"*

*"If you're not running, you're wrong!"* Every word seemed to be uttered with precise pitch.

"You call that *running?*" mocked one of the drill sergeants.

The rapid sound of weighted boots on the pavement came together in succession with heavy breathing and grunts.

About sixty breathless trainees between the ages of sixteen and thirty-two stood in formation. Amid the smell of perspiration, duffel backs still on our backs, we gazed at the monarchical presence before us: Skin glistening, our three drill sergeants stared at us with scowls and annoyance, as if we were to blame for the heat.

At 5'7" tall, salt-and-pepper haired Drill Sergeant Yelman, the eldest, peered at us—razor sharp eyes slicing us to pieces. With breakfast now tied up in knots, I held my breath until he spoke.

"Platoon, I am Drill Sergeant Yelman. Drill Sergeant Dundee is to my right, Drill Sergeant Hutchinson to my left. You are Delta Company Warlords."

He paced across the platoon in short rapid steps and continued. "From now on, when you're in formation and hear atten-*tion!*' you will repeat these words: *"We are the Warlords—the best by far. We smoke all the others like a cheap cigar. Motivation, dedication, that's our style. It's been that way for a long, long, while. Drive on, drill sergeant, drive on, argh-hoo!"*

He stopped pacing and resumed his introduction. "We'll make one of you platoon leader and four of you squad leaders. You will wear stripes on your left sleeve. You will be responsible for the members of your platoon or squad. Handle their complaints. We don't want to hear them. When it's time to clean the barracks, you supervise. You do not clean. If you're caught cleaning or doing anything we think is stupid, you'll be stripped of your stripes. Drill Sergeant Dundee is passing around a list of items you need to buy at the P/X. Finance personnel are here. After formation, you will receive an advance on your pay for what's on the list only. We know the cost of everything. Put your money in your right cargo pocket, and leave your gear where you are standing. Drill Sergeant Dundee will march you to and from the P/X."

Of the three, Drill Sergeant Hutchinson was the most muscular and quietest, the one who would later generate the least amount of fear. At six feet tall, he was a black man with a shiny bald head and empathetic brown eyes.

"Once in the barracks, you will fold every item the way you are told to fold it. No originality here. Your wall and foot lockers will be inspected. We have rulers. If something is a millimeter off, it will be knocked down. You'll do it until you get it right," resumed Drill Sergeant Yelman.

By the time he finished, Drill Sergeant Dundee, a thin, 5'10" white man with a deep cleft in his chin, had passed by every squad, sneering or scoffing at some trainees.

From the corner of my eye, I could see him approaching—highly polished jump boots moving slow, intentional. He stopped in front of me and stared. *Don't look at him.*

My hands became clammy; my heart beat faster as he inched closer. I could see the pores on his face, smell the aftershave, and just about taste the cigarette on his breath.

Gritting my teeth, clenching my jaw, I breathed in slow intervals hoping not to reveal the rise in my chest.

Finally, without a word, he marched towards the front of the platoon. "Right face!" he commanded. "Forward march!" In his baritone voice, he called out cadence. "Everywhere I go there's a drill sergeant there. . . ."

I knew he would be the toughest.

At the P/X, Drill Sergeant Dundee warned, "You have thirty minutes. Don't make me wait. This is not a date. If you're late, you will drop. Go!"

The list contained toiletry essentials, locks for our wall and foot lockers, a shoeshine kit, and a black marker to label our clothes.

Uniformity was key, including the undergarments—white cotton elastic-band underwear that reached your belly button, as well as white cotton padded bras with thick straps and padding that would make your breasts sweat.

I removed two bras from a rack, placed them in my basket, and looked at Buck, the soldier who happened to be on my right. "This is gross."

"I know. It looks like my grandmother's underwear," she replied.

"Not mine."

She laughed. "That's a good one. Did ya get everything?"

"Yeah. Wanna head out together?"

We left the well-lit P/X and found some of the trainees waiting in the shade. *I hope the rest get here fast.*

"It's 1053 hours. There are seven minutes left!" barked Drill Sergeant Dundee. Turning to those present, his eyes darkened as he glared. "You better go get the rest, or you will all drop."

Nobody moved.

"What are you standing there looking stupid for?" He looked at his watch. "Six minutes, fifteen seconds. *Go!*"

We ran inside fearfully and found the remaining members within the allotted time.

At the barracks, he began his speech. "The first two

squads will sleep downstairs, and the last two will sleep upstairs. Each of you will sound off in numerical order, beginning with number one. Remember it. After you pick up your gear, go to the bunks on the right hand side first—the bottom bunk on the farthest end will be number one. Number two will be on top, and so on. Your bunkmate will be your buddy. You go everywhere together. Drill Sergeant Hutchinson will tell you how to get your items squared away. Get it right. Nobody wants to get red in the face when they look at your drawers. When I say, 'Fall out,' you will begin to sound off. Fall out!"

I was assigned to the first floor, first bunk, and top bed on the left hand side. My buddy Surgener was from Newark, New Jersey, a city about 15 miles from my hometown. For the earlier part of basic training, she had been named squad leader, until her stripes were pulled for having filled her canteen with orange soda. I was then named squad leader.

Before the sun rose, we performed physical training on a daily basis—rain or shine. Failure and surrender were not options, rather character flaws that had to be eliminated.

Rifle drills were conducted in full uniform, wool socks, and combat boots while jogging in place with weapons overhead. Drops of sweat dripped from our foreheads, armpits, necks, places I'd never thought would produce sweat, such as inside the ears and nostrils. It seemed insane—until we met Heartbreak Hill, a steep inclination at the end of a five-mile run.

Cheering myself on, I had begun to ascend the hill when I saw Lawrence struggling to my left. Teamwork had been stressed.

"Come on, Lawrence," I said between breaths.

She looked defeated. "I can't, Torres."

"Yes, you can!" I moved beside her.

Lawrence was dragging her feet. "I'm about to pass out."

"No, you're not. You're almost there. Come on."

Some trainees passed us. "No, go. Don't stay for me."

I went behind her and placed my hands on the small of her back. "Just keep moving. I'll keep pushing."

"Okay, Torres."

We continued in that manner until we made it to the end.

Slowing to a walk, hands on my hips, I said, "See? You did it!"

Her eyes expressed gratitude. "'Cause of you, Torres."

"'Cause of you too, Lawrence."

Confidence and camaraderie grew that night—the timing was perfect for the following morning's training exercise: bayonet training.

Drill Sergeant Yelman commanded, "Platoon, when I ask, 'What is the purpose of rifle bayonet training?' you will answer: 'To kill, to kill, to kill without mercy!' and you will strike the dummy in front of you. When I ask, 'What makes the grass grow green?' you will call out: 'Guts, Drill Sergeant, guts!' When I ask, 'What makes the flowers bloom?' you will shout: 'Blood, Drill Sergeant, blood!' Ready?"

"Yes, Drill Sergeant!"

"Platoon, what is the purpose of rifle bayonet training?"

"To kill, to kill, to kill without mercy—*argh!*"

After the words became second nature, it was time for lunch. Waiting on line for chow meant you were either standing at parade rest with eyes facing front or doing push-ups, but *never* talking. Food was something you always craved. Kitchen police duty was a task every trainee had to complete.

My turn came on the day of the Victory Tower, a seventy-foot construction containing challenging exercises. I was upset that I would have to miss it, but knowing Buck was afraid of heights, I asked if she wanted to switch turns.

"Gee, that'd be great! But what are you gonna tell Drill Sergeant Yelman?"

"Well, I'm not gonna tell him you're afraid. He might make you go. I'll say I really wanna go, and you're doing me a favor."

After ensuring my uniform and boots were squared away, I marched to Drill Sergeant Yelman's office. A rustle of papers came from the room as I halted outside the slightly ajar door. I knocked twice and waited at parade rest.

The papers stopped moving. "Who's there?" asked Yelman, hint of annoyance evident.

"Private Torres, Drill Sergeant."

"What do you want Private Torres?"

"Drill Sergeant, Private Torres requests permission to enter."

"Enter."

I marched into his office and stood at attention.

Seated behind his metal desk in front of a window, he looked up with curiosity. "Yes, Private Torres?"

"Drill Sergeant, Private Torres requests permission to speak."

"Speak. . .at ease," he said, placing his paperwork face down.

"Drill Sergeant, I have KP duty tomorrow, but it's the day

of the Victory Tower, and I really want to go. I spoke with Private Buck, who hasn't had KP duty yet. She's willing to do me the favor and go in my place, and I'll go when it's her turn."

He appeared offended. "And who said you could do that?"

I hadn't expected that question. My next set of words had to be chosen wisely in case I ruined my chances of going to the tower. "No one, Drill Sergeant. That's why I'm asking you."

"It sounds like you made the decision on your own."

*Oh, boy.* I said nothing, but hoped the black rotary phone on his desk would ring.

"Who said you could ask her, Private Torres?"

"No one, Drill Sergeant. I just asked her." The Victory Tower seemed further away.

"That was your idea?" he asked in a condescending manner.

"Yes, Drill Sergeant."

"Who said you could have any ideas?"

*Oh man, I'm not getting anywhere.* "No one, Drill Sergeant. I just thought that, since I really wanted to go, she might do me the favor if I asked."

"What if she wants to do it? Did you ever think of that?"

"I asked her, but she knows that I want to do it more than she does, and she's willing to switch with me."

Exasperated, he lifted his hands. "Private Torres, tell her to come in here."

"Yes, Drill Sergeant." I returned to attention and marched out.

"He wants to see you, Buck," I said.

"What for?" she asked nervously, eyes shifting behind her

government-issued birth-control glasses (BCGs).

I shrugged. "I guess he wants to see if it's true."

I couldn't eavesdrop because doing so would be sure to get me in trouble; instead I sat to wait on my old wooden foot locker.

"Well? What'd he say?" I asked her a few minutes later.

"He said he'll talk to the other drill sergeants tomorrow."

"Why? He's the head drill sergeant."

"I don't know, Torres. I'm sorry. I did what I could."

"I know. Thanks for trying, Buck. I guess we'll see."

The following morning I reported for KP duty in the steamy mess hall kitchen, topped off the orange juice containers, and stood behind the bacon tray to serve it.

After breakfast, I sat near the kitchen sink to peel potatoes, clangs of pots and pans nearby. With every peel, I became angrier for missing the Victory Tower, muttering under my breath.

All of a sudden a pair of highly shined jump boots stopped before me.

I looked up to see Drill Sergeant Dundee. *Now what?*

"Let's go, Private Torres. Private Buck is here to relieve you from KP duty."

I couldn't believe it! "Yes, Drill Sergeant," I said, rising while scanning for Buck to exchange a simple smile of gratitude.

The Victory Tower contained a tall net to climb up, and onto multiple styles of rope, which crossed from one end to the other. On one end of the tower, some trainees rappelled down a wooden plank while a buddy stood on the ground holding the other end of their rope. I couldn't wait to do it all and quickly joined a team.

The four of us looked up. "So what do we do?" asked Icker, a trainee from another platoon.

"I think we should sit on your shoulders since you're the tallest, and reach up to climb onto the rung," I said to Icker, who stood 5'8".

"Yeah, that's a good idea. From there, we can pull the next person up and keep moving in the same way," Icker replied.

"Okay, who goes first? She's the shortest," asked Zullo, who pointed to Mari, her buddy from fourth platoon.

"Yeah, but I'm not the strongest, just the easiest to pull up," offered Mari.

"You're right, you can go third. I might get tired as we go further up," said Icker.

"Well, you're just an inch taller than me, so we can take turns," suggested Zullo, who then turned to me. "You wanna go first, Torres?"

From that point on, we began our ascent. Once we got to the top, we high-fived each other and quickly moved to the rappelling line. Our exercise had ended, but not its lesson in teamwork.

"How ya feeling, Private?" asked Drill Sergeant Stern, a highly motivated Master Jumper Airborne Ranger.

"Outstanding, Drill Sergeant!"

"Ooh-rah!"

After reviewing rappelling instructions, he asked, "You ready?" His light green eyes searched mine for signs of fear.

"Yes, Drill Sergeant!" He raised his thumb at my buddy below.

My feet landed on the wooden plank with a hard thud. I

felt invincible. It had been a pure adrenalin rush, and each leap brought greater euphoria.

By the day's end, our confidence had skyrocketed. We could've sworn there was nothing we couldn't do—until we heard about the gas chamber scheduled for the following day.

The purpose of that exercise was to assure us that the protective masks worked, while giving us an idea of what to expect in a nuclear, biological, or chemical environment.

With masks donned, we lined up outside the gas chamber entrance.

"Next!" shouted the drill sergeant.

Being third in a group of six, I followed, hoping everyone would comply with the orders given inside. In the center of the dark, hot, smoky room stood the chamber sergeant, wearing his mask, beckoning us to walk toward him.

We stopped in front of him in nervous anticipation. He gave the order to remove our masks. I removed mine, held my breath, and kept my eyes somewhat closed. Immediately, I felt the stinging on my face.

"Remove your mask," said the sergeant.

I opened my eyes completely to see who he was speaking to. It was the trainees that were fifth and sixth in line. They shook their heads.

"Remove your masks, Privates!"

I was pissed. The stinging had spread to my eyes, and my arms felt like there were creepy crawlies on them. I didn't know how much longer I could hold my breath.

One private unmasked, but not the other.

"Private!" shouted the sergeant. She unmasked.

He walked to the first trainee. "Name, rank, social security number." She provided the information, breathing in the air, and began coughing. The second trainee had the same response.

At last it was my turn. Opening my mouth was the equivalent of getting slapped hard in the face with a burning hand. The gas was horrid! The stinging felt like I was being whipped with flames. All I could hope for was that the others would follow through.

They did; finally, he opened the door.

The stinging on my skin increased, making me want to scratch it, but I remembered a training sergeant had suggested flapping our arms. The air would bring some relief, but scratching would worsen it.

My eyes stung and teared. I widened them to expose them to air. When my nose started to run, I recalled an instructor's remark that exposure to gas opened your pores. The effects would be over in less than an hour.

Bivouac was next. We learned basic rifle skills and handling, fired numerous weapons, and met our best friend—the M16A1 rifle. We dug trenches around two-man tents, curled up in our sleeping bags, ate MREs, and dug holes for our necessities. Through mud and rain, we'd march to the next field exercise at port arms, a poncho over our sixty-pound rucksacks.

In this last training phase, there were two qualifications: weapons and grenades. The former was scored by the number of hits on your target: Marksman (23/40), Sharpshooter (30/40) or Expert (36 or more). The latter required throwing the grenade a certain distance. Everyone was tense. No one wanted to go home a failure or be recycled into the next class.

That day was cloudy. A group of us was lined up beside foxholes, plugs in our ears, weapons at sling arms, waiting for the range master's instructions. Range flags were raised and commands followed: "Hold your fire!", "Commence firing!", and "Cease fire!"

Weapons jammed; clearing them took seconds. Hearing shots fired instilled concentration on the silhouette targets that randomly popped up.

Afterward, we sat on aluminum bleachers to wait for the results.

Then I heard it over the megaphone: "Torres, 34." I sighed in relief. However, others didn't, and though we were sad to see fellow trainees go, we knew our focus had to remain on the next qualification—grenades.

Drill Sergeant Cano began, "The M67 Fragmentation Hand Grenade weighs 14 ounces. It can be thrown 30 to 35 meters by the average soldier."

Things had become more of a challenge for me. For some reason, my right shoulder had collapsed due to heavy rain on previous nights, causing me to use my left hand to qualify.

I entered the bunker wondering how I'd do. Drill Sergeant Cano said, "Private Torres, throw the first grenade."

Spreading my feet, I cupped the steel sphere body of the grenade, pulled the pin, and threw it as hard as I could. "Grenade!" I shouted, crouching low in the bunker.

Drill Sergeant Cano stood up. "As you were, Private. Now the second one."

Moments later my results were evident: I had passed.

Graduation day came, and I marched my squad forward while Mom, Marlene, and George watched proudly. The platoon went back to the barracks for our belongings.

Each drill sergeant delivered encouraging speeches. Such is the process of basic training—being broken down to be built back up.

Drill Sergeant Yelman boomed, "There is one special recognition award for superior performance. This individual soldier has been a true leader and will have a bright military career. She has superseded all military expectations while displaying perseverance, courage, and motivation."

I wondered who it would be.

Suddenly, I heard, "Private Torres, front and center."

I was waiting to see who the soldier was when Buck nudged me, "Hey, Torres, that's you. Go!"

Bewildered, I stood before them.

Drill Sergeant Yelman looked me in the eye. "Congratulations, Private Torres."

"Thank you, Drill Sergeant."

Drill Sergeant Dundee and Drill Sergeant Hutchinson followed.

In the end, forty-two trainees graduated and earned the priceless sobriquet—United States soldier. I could not recall a prouder moment on the ride home. At last, I relished in my success.

# 9

# Semper Fi

JUST AS ROLLO HAD SUGGESTED, I enrolled in the ROTC program in the fall of 1986. An officer's job in the military consists of mundane administrative duties I dislike: paperwork, planning, and meetings. Although being enlisted involved more physical work, it had been fun. I enjoyed the no-nonsense approach of my enlisted brothers and sisters. Aside from the greater respect and pay an officer receives, I didn't find any benefit, so once the semester ended I discontinued the program.

George and I had reached our one-year anniversary without intimacy that October. I was thankful that he never pressured me; I wasn't ready. His patience confirmed the old adage: True love waits.

Spring sped; my Advanced Individual Training, Motor Transport Operator course in Fort Leonard Wood, Missouri, would begin on June 25, 1987, a week after George's twenty-first birthday. To celebrate it, we drove to Ay Caramba's, a Mexican eatery down the block from Tower Records in New York City.

Quite an alluring man, George wore clothes that complemented the muscularity in his strong legs and chest: gray dress slacks and a powder blue long-sleeved shirt underneath a black blazer. To please him, I wore what he loved to see me in: a form-fitting black leather mini-skirt, a loose short-sleeved leopard-print suede blouse, and high heels.

At the dinner table, he removed his blazer and rolled up his sleeves, revealing smooth, enticing forearms. I reached out to touch him. "Happy Birthday."

"Thank you Jewels," he smiled, giving my hand a firm squeeze.

We drank a couple of what were called Ridiculous Margaritas—so huge that the waiter wouldn't bring them unless we ordered food. Of course, we stuffed our faces with chips, salsa, and *quesadillas*.

"Holy cow! He wasn't kidding," I said after the waiter set the margaritas down on the table.

As we sipped the drinks, I wondered about his short-term plans. "You leaving work soon?"

"Hopefully. . .I've been looking around to see when they'll be giving the police exams. Since I want to be a corrections officer, I could go to the sheriff's department, work the prisons, courts, street, whatever. . .but the tests are hard."

"Not for you. You'll do it."

"Thanks, Jewels." He grabbed a napkin to wipe guacamole from my face.

"You can dress me, but you can't take me out, huh?" I joked.

He bit into his *quesadilla*. "Nah, not me. I'll dress you *and* take you out."

I left to the bathroom with the intention of having the waiter approach our table with the restaurant's mariachi in tow. Minutes later, the group arrived holding a dish of fried vanilla ice cream drizzled in chocolate sauce, topped with whipped cream, slices of fresh banana, and a glowing candle. They began singing George the birthday song while he grinned broadly.

As usual, time flew when we were together, and after several hours, with palates pleased and love amiss, we decided to return home.

The night couldn't have been better as we strolled to the car, hand in hand, talking, laughing, oblivious to the busy city sights and sounds around us. The cool breeze blew my hair softly, bringing with it the scent of George's piny cologne: Polo by Ralph Lauren.

Driving back home in Mom's Volkswagen with a comfortable buzz, my hand rested on his strong thigh, as was my norm. Listening to soft music on the radio, I turned to watch him drive: firm jawline, high cheekbones and focused eyes, personifying manly confidence. We relished stopping at long, red lights where we'd kiss until honking horns brought us back to earth.

"You wanna park somewhere?" he asked on the Jersey side.

"Yeah," I said, still high from his scent, the taste in my mouth—a pleasing mixture of tequila and mint.

We drove to River Road in Edgewater, parked the car in a spot overlooking Manhattan, and turned it off, rotating the ignition key slightly to let the music play. We began kissing again, reclining the right passenger seat as George leaned his body over mine.

Almost two years had passed without us forming an intimate bond. *Semper Fidelis*, the Marine Corps' *Always Faithful* motto, fit George's beliefs to those around him. I loved, admired, and respected him and wanted to express my love for him.

The windows fogged. The temperature in the car rose while he whispered in my ear. The sound of his husky voice, his hands on my body, and the feel of his manhood through his dress slacks made me want him more.

Although I was nervous and doubted my emotional readiness, I knew George was the right one, and that weekend was the perfect time.

The longing in my eyes was clear when I stopped and looked at him. "George, I don't want to do it like this with you. I wanna take you to Atlantic City for your birthday."

As easy as that, we regrouped and smiled at one another, letting out a slight chuckle at the sight in front of us—the New York City skyline over the Hudson River at sunrise. Interlocking his fingers with mine, he gave my hand a gentle squeeze. At that moment, I loved him more.

Around 5:00 a.m., we stopped at Mom's. I awoke her while George waited in the kitchen. "Ma, can me and George take your car to Atlantic City? We'll be back tomorrow."

"Yes."

"Thanks, Ma."

"Is he here?"

"Yes, in the kitchen. I'm gonna get some clothes."

After putting on her slippers and robe, she greeted him. "*Hola, mi niño.* How are you?"

"Good, Daisy. And you?"

"Good. Julia says you're going to Atlantic City."

"Yes, we want to go for my birthday. Is that okay with you?"

"Yes, of course." She looked at him tenderly. "I know she's in good hands. How has your birthday been so far?"

George, ever chivalrous, said, "Thank you, Daisy. . .my birthday's been great!"

"I'm glad to hear that. You have a long drive ahead of you. Let me make you some espresso," Mom offered.

Later, we left to George's house, where he told his mom we were going away and packed some clothes.

The long ride to Atlantic City was full of engaging conversation, something we never fell short of. George liked to drive with his hand, palm down, under my thigh; it felt nice to know that we were connected somehow.

The weekend weather seemed as if it was going to stay the same—sun beaming in a cloudless sky. Atlantic City's welcome sign and elaborate casinos greeted us. We chose the first hotel we saw and checked in. Seeing the inviting, king-sized bed in the cozy room made us realize how exhausted we were.

"Okay to take a nap first?" I asked.

"Of course. I was just gonna ask you the same thing." George drew the thick curtains together.

After removing our dress clothes but remaining in our undergarments, we crashed on the bed, curling into each other's warmth under the comforter. We must've fallen asleep when our heads made contact with the pillows.

About six hours later, I opened my eyes to see George staring at me, lying on his side, one hand underneath his head, the other in front of his chest. He smiled, "Hey, there, sleepy head."

Wondering if my breath stank, I covered my mouth. "You've been watching me?"

"Yup. Jewels, even when you drool, you look beautiful," he laughed.

"Get outta here. I don't drool."

"How do you know? You're sleeping."

Chuckling, I said, "Stop kidding! . . . It's nice to wake up to you."

"Thank you. I feel the same. It's nice to wake up to me, too." That was George—witty, quick with comebacks. "I'm joking," he added. "It's great to wake up and see you."

I smiled, "Mind if I take a shower first?"

"No, go ahead."

I got up, giving him a peck on the forehead.

As the water from the shower head sprayed over my body, I hoped we could make love without any hindrances. I struggled with the thought that the memory of my rape would return. Would it get the best of me? Would our moment be ruined? I didn't know, but I had to try.

George was not aware of my rape. Although he would've been supportive, I still did not want to acknowledge it, and I believed it'd hurt him if I shared it. If I did tell him, I didn't know if he'd seek vengeance, which might've ruined his future in law enforcement before it'd begun.

Wrapped in a towel, I opened the door. "You're next, stinky."

"Ha, ha."

After dressing, I sat on the bed brushing my hair in front of the television. Twenty minutes later, George emerged bare-chested, towel around his waist. I sighed, breathing in his intoxicating scent. A couple of water spots remained on the hairless chest I loved.

Putting my hairbrush down, I grabbed a hand towel and stood before him. "Let me get this."

"Oh yeah? Anything else?" he joked.

I laughed nervously, glancing at him. When his inviting eyes met mine, my heart fluttered. We leaned into each other and began kissing. I stroked his back, feeling the strength of his muscles from the nape of his neck to the small of his back.

When our passion increased, he took my hands in his and stopped me. "Are you sure?"

"Yes," I whispered.

And just as tenderly, he began removing my clothes; the two of us lay down as I took off his towel.

When our thirst had been quenched, he looked at me, eyes happy, relaxed. "How do you feel?" he asked.

"Great. You?"

"Outstanding. You sure you're okay?"

"Yup, but I'm starving."

Perhaps I had worried for naught; there hadn't been any intrusive thoughts. How wonderful it felt to be truly loved and to be able to reciprocate it.

We had lunch a couple of blocks down from the hotel—warm bread and butter, steak and potatoes, vanilla ice cream, and chocolate cake. With contented stomachs, we walked through the casinos.

"Wanna go to the beach?" George asked.

"Sure."

Lacing our sneakers and throwing them over our shoulders, we strolled hand in hand on the warm sand with our pant legs rolled up, splashing one another along the way. Seagulls cawed in the soft wind as the smell of the ocean salt hovered.

"Let's sit down," I suggested.

Having had a more than satisfactory day, we took a nap in each other's arms.

By the time we awoke, it was getting dark, and we made our way back to the room, grabbing hot dogs and soda from a vendor. We didn't want the night to end. Others' footsteps on the boardwalk were no longer appealing, nor were the beats from a teen's boom box.

In the room, we watched television in comfortable silence until we prepared for bed at midnight. Before we fell asleep, we began making love once more.

This time, however, it was different.

Tears welled up in my eyes, and like a vile, unpredictable illness, sick memories came flooding back without remorse, wreaking havoc. I repeated George's name in my head hoping it'd take control of my mind.

It hurt to know I was still waging that war alone. I felt defeated. I wondered if I'd be brave enough to make love with George again, or brave enough not to. But how could I stop a negative thought from entering my mind?

The writing on the wall became crystal clear. Regardless of his exceedingly special ways or the love we shared, two years had not been long enough. My heart was heavy when I fell asleep.

On our return trip the following morning, I tried to be happy, but that black cloud hovered. The man who loved me unconditionally was driving relaxed, his right hand resting once again under my left thigh. I reached out to caress his cheek. *If he only knew. . .*

Not wanting to talk for fear of crying, I said, "If you don't mind, I'm gonna take a nap."

"Okay. Go ahead."

Before I closed my eyes, I recorded the last image in my mind: George's loving face. *Please let me fall asleep—no more bad thoughts.*

A few hours later, he woke me up. "We're here."

We greeted Mom, who expressed thanks for bringing me back safe. Afterwards, I drove him home so he could rest.

"We don't have a lot of time left," he said in resignation.

"No," I said sadly, knowing the weight of those words. "Let's spend as much time as we can together every day when we get out of work." We kissed good-bye.

I watched him go up the stairs, and fought the tears that were coming. There'd be enough time for them.

We did as promised, used every minute wisely, laughing, talking, eating, making love—but in the back of my mind, doubts remained. I wondered when, and how often, they would recur. When bad memories crept up on me, I tried to fight them, but I wasn't always victorious. I hated it. I couldn't give him my all.

George asked me one day that week, "Will you be the mother of my children?"

Knowing he wanted to have girls, I answered, "Only if it's a boy." That was the gist of our relationship. George always wanted to give me more than I could accept.

The days flew. I called him the morning of my departure. "I'm leaving."

"Okay, be safe. Try to find time to write."

"I will."

"See you in August, Jewels."

"Good-bye, George," I said, with dreaded resignation.

# *IO*

# Consequences

A S IF ON CUE, A CAR HORN BLARED at 0400 hours when the call ended. I separated the narrow white blinds of my bedroom window and peered through them. It was rare to see anyone awake that early on a Sunday morning, especially on 18th Street in Union City, where I'd been living with Mom between semester breaks.

The dim morning sky would brighten up soon—yes, the moment had come to leave things behind. After kissing Mom lightly to avoid waking her, I strapped the green canvas military duffel bag onto my back and locked my bedroom door with the unusual, but lovely, skeleton key.

Stepping outside in my starched camouflage uniform, hat, and polished combat boots, I opened the creaky cab door, hefting my bag onto the vinyl seat of the old green Chevrolet.

Soft jazz emerged from the radio on our way to Newark

International Airport, while I rolled down the window, imagining the crisp wind lifting the sadness in my heart. When potholes interrupted my thoughts, I shifted my attention to the matter at hand: motor transport training.

At the airport, unknown figures carrying coffee cups moved robotically, dressed in seemingly identical clothing, until it was time for me to board. Content to see my row on the plane empty, I fell asleep.

Over the intercom a few hours later, the captain's voice awoke me as he signaled our descent to Waynesville-St. Robert Regional Airport in Fort Leonard Wood. With my duffel bag beside me, a hailed cab took me to the barracks, where panoramic views of leafy trees and carefree runners brought me the hope that these drill sergeants would be less intimidating than those from basic.

Entering a three-story brick building, I walked up a buffed, fluorescent-lit hallway to an attractive, olive-complexioned Puerto Rican drill sergeant holding a Smokey-the-Bear hat. To his right, sitting behind a metal desk, was a dark-haired, buzz-cut young fellow in BDUs. The scent of fresh showers and after-shave cologne welcomed me. Both men were examining a list of names on a clipboard. Straightening up, the drill sergeant stood at six feet; his name tag read *Reyes*.

"Drill Sergeant Reyes, I'm Private First Class Torres, reporting for duty," I said, retrieving my orders from my cargo pocket.

"Ahem. Good to have you, PFC Torres." His warm, milk-chocolate eyes expressed assurance. "I don't need to see your orders. I have them. Relax. This isn't Basic—you're a soldier now."

*What a relief!* "Thank you, Drill Sergeant."

"There are twenty-nine trainees in your transportation class. PVT Hoover here is one of them." Hoover and I exchanged nods. "He is performing his twelve-hour CQ runner duties. That's Charge of Quarters. Every soldier has them. You're the only female in your class, but not the only one in the building. PFC Allen and PVT Groves are finishing up their mechanic's course with the soldiers on the second floor, who report to a different drill sergeant."

Motioning towards a hallway on the right, he added, "Females sleep on this side of the building. No males are allowed in the females' quarters. Your classmates are on the third floor. Pick any room you want, square it away, secure your gear, and be in formation in ten minutes."

"Yes, Drill Sergeant."

I chose the room in the left corner, where a set of wool blankets and white sheets lay neatly folded over a striped pillow on each steel-framed bunk bed. I quickly made the bottom one.

Before placing my duffel bag inside the rattly wall locker, I withdrew the one item I couldn't leave without—a picture I had taken of George in Atlantic City. Positioning it on the edge of the small Plexiglas mirror, I paused: *I should've told him I loved him.* After attaching the locker key to the dog tags around my neck, I joined the platoon formation at attention.

Drill Sergeant Reyes began speaking in a clear baritone voice. "Platoon, at ease. I am Drill Sergeant Reyes, the one in charge of these quarters. If there are any problems, see me. Today is Sunday. Enjoy your time off. You will get your first weekend pass next month if all of you perform to standard.

You'll get the second pass before your graduation. Are we clear so far?"

"Yes, Drill Sergeant!" we shouted.

"Good. Formations will be at 0500 hours for PT, 0630 for chow, and 0745 for training. At that time you will be turned over to your training drill sergeants for daily instruction. See you at PT tomorrow. Platoon, attention! Fall out."

The next morning, Drill Sergeant Hill, a 5'10" white guy with an angular jaw and a lanky build, stood before us. "Me and Drill Sergeant Walker will be your training drill sergeants. You will do what we say." The fixed stare in his caramel-colored eyes was piercing; the beauty mark on his cheekbone accentuated his point. *There goes my hope for less intimidation.*

"We will take you to and from instruction. Do not be late for formation. If there is any soldier here who does not know how to drive stick, raise your hand."

Not wanting to be the only one, I was hesitant to raise mine, but I knew there was no way around it. Suddenly, a soldier's arm rose to my far right; mine followed.

"What's your name, soldier?" asked Drill Sergeant Hill.

"Vazquez, Drill Sergeant."

"Come with me."

Raising what looked like a longer version of a musical conductor's stick, Drill Sergeant Walker pointed it at me. "You!"

*Oh, no!* I clenched my jaw and gritted my teeth.

Drill Sergeant Walker, a mid-thirties black man, had a presence larger than his 5'4" appearance. His ebony eyes behind thick plastic-framed glasses challenged when he bellowed, "Follow me!" as he walked away with a casual swagger.

Hurriedly, I left formation to catch up to him, but when I

saw he had entered the front passenger side of a Jeep vehicle, I felt doomed. I didn't even know how to start one, never mind drive it.

In an irritated manner, he spoke from the corner of his mouth. "Get in."

And so I did.

"You have half an hour. Remember three things: accelerator, clutch, stick."

My lesson began with him barking out orders. "Jeep in neutral, right foot brake, left foot clutch, stick in first gear, release brake, right foot accelerator and ease off the clutch at the same time. . .move it!"

There were so many orders that I was surprised I got the thing started. Fear had made me get it right, but every time I didn't, he tapped me on the knee with the stick. I freewheeled; he tapped. I grinded gears; he tapped. I choked the engine; he tapped. Tap, tap, tap—there was no way around it. But thirty minutes later, I was driving stick.

Within a few weeks, we met our standards, moving up in vehicle size from a Jeep to a Cut-Vee, to a deuce and a half, to a five ton, and finally to the tractor-trailer—the meat of our training. In order to graduate, the latter had to be reversed between cones in three attempts.

The day of my final exam occurred on an extremely stifling day as I waited behind the wheel of an idling truck. With my clammy hands on the thin power-steering wheel, the hair in my hat drenched in sweat, and the back of my neck warm to the touch, the anxiety in my stomach grew as each minute passed.

When I saw Drill Sergeant Hill march toward my vehicle,

my queasy stomach turned into a convoluted knot. My hands clammed up further, slipping off the wheel. In one swift move, he stepped onto the metal footstep near the driver's side door, grabbed the window bars, and blocked my side-view mirror.

"I'm ready," he challenged.

*Oh, God.* I was too afraid to ask him to move.

Discreetly, I wiped my hands on my cargo pants and began the reversal process with slow movements, using the limited view I had of the passenger side mirror, ensuring that none of the eighteen wheels would touch the cones—not even by a sliver. *Keep calm.* When I could no longer see, I estimated.

Although we had three chances, I knew I had to do it right the first time or my frustration would be my demise. Once done, I put the gear in park and remained staring ahead. Seeing Drill Sergeant Hill's shocked reaction out of my peripheral vision was classic. His mouth was agape, eyes widened, brows lifted.

Then I heard the incredulity in his voice. "Te-rez, why didn't you ask me to move?"

Slowly, I turned to him. "I knew I could do it without asking you, Drill Sergeant."

He shook his head and walked away. I would've laughed out loud if I'd had the nerve.

As I lay down on my bunk that night, I knew the training was coming to end, which meant my relationship with George would also. I didn't want it to be over, but it was inescapable. I wondered how I could break up with George when an idea came to me during the final weekend pass.

It involved Dakota Bauer, our nineteen-year-old platoon leader from Illinois, who looked like a dirty-blond Elvis Presley with hazel eyes. As a leader, he commanded us fairly; as a young man, he was courteous.

Around midnight on that cloudless Saturday night, a group of us were returning to the barracks from the non-commissioned officer's club. Our loud laughter and shouts decreased as we drew closer. Two of the guys took their last cigarette puffs, flicking them into the garbage can before entering, while the other two shuffled into the barracks.

I stayed behind; it was now or never. Spitting out my minty gum, I stopped outside Bauer's window, calling out his name and beginning a serenade while swaying and using my hands.

"Hey," he said, smiling. "What are you doing?"

"Bauer, will you marry me?" I asked without preface.

Mouth open, brows raised, he asked, "*Marry* you?"

"Yeah."

The outdoor lamps lit his broadening smile. "Yes."

"Okay."

I don't know why he consented to marry me when all we'd had were pleasant talks, but I must've figured him out right. His wholesome, rural upbringing had made him a young man who believed that marriage could be that simple.

I entered my room, having solved the situation with George, who had too much pride to chase a girl. I knew he wouldn't call me again when he'd heard I had returned home with a fiancé.

As cruel as it was, it was the only way my young, damaged mind could find a way out. I had no intention of following through with either relationship, and I failed to recognize the pain I'd cause through such insensitive behavior, but I could not face George. What reason would I have given?

If I had said that I was not ready for continued intimacy, he would've accepted it. But then what? I'd have the reminder that he only knew half of the truth. It wasn't fair to him any way I looked at it. There was one thing I was certain of: I was not ready to acknowledge my rape so I had to accept the consequences.

Around 1630 hours the following Sunday afternoon, I was sitting on my bed, doing a crossword puzzle, when the CQ runner called out from the hall.

"Torres! Bauer wants to see you."

"Okay. I'll be there in a few minutes," I shouted.

I tidied up my quarters and met Bauer. "Hey," I said.

"Hi, Torres. Do you want to go to the mess hall with me for supper?"

"Sure."

It was a lovely day; the scent of freshly manicured lawns, and the sun's warmth made an ideal combination for our walk there in shorts, t-shirts, and sneakers. There weren't many soldiers present; our weekend pass wasn't over until 1800 hours, but on occasion the clang of dishes and the sound of flowing tap water reminded us we were in the chow hall.

The buffet bar was filled with pasta, meatballs, sausage and peppers, mashed potatoes, gravy, chocolate cake, and orange Jell-O. Near the end, baskets of bread and dishes with butter packets were spread out next to the sodas and milk machines.

I put some spaghetti on my plate, scooped up meatballs in

marinara sauce, and sprinkled them with Parmesan cheese. Grabbing a dessert plate of chocolate cake and filling two glasses with soda, I went to a corner booth to wait for Bauer. Since I didn't want him to see me eat spaghetti, I started cutting it into pieces.

"I do that too!" he exclaimed when he neared our table.

Lifting my fork, I laughed, "Get outta here!"

"Yeah, that's swell," he smiled, eyes revealing flecks of gold.

"Great minds think alike."

"That's right." Between bites, he asked, "Did you mean what you said last night?"

"Yeah."

"Well, I'd like to meet your mom. Will she be here for graduation?"

"No, she's gotta work."

"My parents will be here. You can meet them then."

"Okay."

"When can I meet your mom?" he asked, scooping up the last of his Jell-O.

"Hold on. I gotta get milk."

When I returned, I replied, "You can fly back with me to Jersey."

"Okay. That's swell. I'll tell my parents."

We finished our meals, left our trays in the washing area, and headed back.

"What are you going to do now?" he asked.

"I'm gonna take a nap."

"Okay, I'll see you tomorrow at PT."

The feeling of dread lay in my stomach, but the die had

been cast.

The final week breezed by, and on August 28, we had our graduation ceremony. It was satisfying to know that I had succeeded in a field where men reigned, but it seemed ironic that I lacked the gumption to reveal the truth to George.

Bauer introduced me to his parents, and after wishing us a safe flight, we headed to New Jersey, but not before calling Mom to say I had a surprise.

Spotting her curls near the gate, her smile turned to a grimace when she noticed I was walking arm in arm with a stranger. Her trepidation grew when she realized I had come home with "an American boy," as she described him.

"Hi, Ma. This is Dakota. We're getting married."

"Hello, ma'am. Pleased to meet you," he said, nodding and extending his hand.

Ever transparent, Mom looked as if she were about to cry. She offered a muted hello and briefly shook his hand. "Okay, let's go."

Her guess at my "surprise" had been that I'd gotten married, and she hadn't been far off. I knew she was very disappointed when she raised the radio volume on the ride home.

"He's not sleeping with you in your room?" she asked rhetorically when we arrived.

"No, of course not."

A measure of relief filled her face as she turned to Dakota. "You sleep in Julia room; she sleep with me."

He nodded, "Yes, ma'am."

The next day we visited Marissa, who was still dating Jack, George's best friend. There, I began spreading the news that Dakota was my fiancé. George found out I had returned but did not call me.

One night that week, I came home from the movies with Dakota to find Mom sitting on a kitchen chair, head downcast. "What's wrong?" I asked.

The fresh lemon scent indicated she had just finished mopping the kitchen floor, but music wasn't playing, as was her cleaning custom. She looked up, pained expression on her face seeking answers. "We need to talk," she said in a serious tone.

"Can you excuse us?" I asked Dakota.

His steps were soft on the linoleum floor as he headed to my room.

"Why did you do that to George?" she asked.

I wondered where the subject had come from. "Do what?"

Using my nickname, Mom began, "Aurorita, you don't play with a man's emotions."

"I'm not *playing*," I snapped. It irked me that she had her own assumptions about why I had broken up with George.

"He's such a nice guy. I like him a lot."

I was affronted that she was more concerned about George's feelings than my obvious, odd behavior. "So marry him!"

We did not discuss it again.

I commuted that fall semester, having registered for classes in the New Brunswick and Newark campuses. Dakota stayed at home while I was at school; sometimes we went out on weekends.

It wasn't until we were returning from New York City one sunny afternoon about a week later that the realization of my marriage proposal struck home.

Dakota suddenly asked, "So when do you want to get married?"

Having avoided the subject since AIT, and not wanting to disclose the truth, I blurted, "In six months."

"Okay. I'll transfer to your unit, so we can drill together."

My head began to spin. *Now what?*

Seated around Marissa's kitchen table, having pizza, the following afternoon, I casually asked, "What do you think of Dakota?"

Knowing exactly what I was fishing for, she rose from her chair, shaking her head and finger as the other hand remained on her hip. "Oh, no, you don't. Don't you try it! I know exactly what you're doing. You got yourself into this mess. You get yourself out."

"You're right," I said looking at her determined brown eyes and firm mouth with a sheepish grin.

I finally got out of it in a cowardly, juvenile manner. I ignored Dakota that week until he finally got the message.

In confused resignation, he said, "I have my ticket to go back home. I'm leaving tomorrow."

"Okay, I'll take you to the airport." That was the end.

I never saw him again.

The battle waging within me made it impossible for me to maintain healthy relationships, even with God. My belief in Him hadn't changed, but I was distant. The shadowy outlines of my rape's effects spiraled me into an abyss. Unfortunately, innocent people also suffered consequences.

# II

# Pancho

ASIDE FROM TURNING TWENTY-ONE, having my photography displayed in two of the art galleries at Mason Gross, and a few photographs published in the Rutgers College Quarterly, my last two years in college were pretty uneventful.

However, during my senior year spring break, an important milestone occurred in California: I visited my father, Francisco de Jesus Torres.

Known as "Pancho," he was the relative whom Mom often compared me to. Rolling her eyes, clearly exasperated, she'd sigh, "Si, *Panchita, si,* just like your father, if he says the moon is black, it's black. You weren't even raised with him. . .but it's in your genes."

She hadn't meant the name "Panchita," the female version of Pancho, as a compliment, but I had accepted it as such. From the snippets I'd heard as a child, my dad seemed intelligent, driven, and gallant, yet unemotional—the former, traits I found appealing; the latter, a necessity at times.

Notorious for being generous and charismatic, he was also a con man. The term *muelero*, a smooth talker with an uncanny ability to maintain a conversation on any subject, suited him well.

Pancho had the wherewithal to conquer anything he wanted, especially women, who only lasted until he eyed his next conquest. It was a pattern that had resulted in a trail of romantic interludes leading him to father eleven children with five women.

His first marriage, to an Italian-American in the United States in 1950, produced Carlo and Dina. Single again between 1957 and 1960, his third and fourth children, Maida and Ileana, came from two different girlfriends in Cuba: Diana and Carmen.

In 1962, my mom married him without knowing he was still involved with Carmen. She gave birth to my sister Marlene in 1963, who became his fifth child. It was no surprise when both women delivered children again in 1964. That October, Carmen had Teresa, his sixth child, and Mom gave birth to my brother Frank, his seventh child, in December.

To complicate things further, while Mom had been pregnant with Frank, and Pancho was still with Carmen, he began an affair with a seventeen-year-old named Ana. When the news was discovered, the minor's father threatened forty-eight-year-old Pancho with imprisonment unless he married his daughter.

Around the same time, my parents were in the midst of filing necessary paperwork to leave Cuba for the United

States. Fearing jail time, he conned Mom to sign divorce papers, having her believe she was signing papers required to expedite the process out of the country.

In 1967, Mom had me, his eighth child. Six months later, Ana had Reinaldo, his ninth child. They were later divorced.

When Pancho immigrated with us to the United States, Mom had already learned of her own divorce, and my parents then went their separate ways: Mom, Abuela, and the three kids moved to New Jersey; Pancho went to California. He later married a young Mexican-American, who bore his tenth and eleventh children, Reiser and Maybeline.

Of all his kids, Mom said I resembled Pancho the most, both personally and physically. Although I hadn't been mindful of it, the physical differences between my siblings and I were evident. Marlene and Frank were fair-skinned and of stocky build, while I was skinny, with long arms and olive skin. It wasn't until one afternoon when I was six years old that those characteristics became suspect.

Mom and her friend, Flor, were sitting around the kitchen table of our apartment drinking espresso and talking. I was heading to the bathroom until I stopped at the sound of my nickname.

"Who does Aurorita look like?" Flor asked.

"Oh, nobody. I saw something in the garbage one day and discovered it was a baby girl. Aurorita was so pretty that I took her home," Mom replied.

I doubled my steps into the bedroom I shared with Marlene, threw myself on my twin bed, and cried. I believed her and began to wonder where I had come from.

As a result, I subconsciously attempted to excel further in

school in order to earn a rightful place in our family. Once I grew older, I explained to Mom the effect her comment had had on me. Although she attributed it to a common idiomatic expression used in Cuba, I cautioned her never to joke like that again.

The first clear memory of my father took root that same year, during Christmas. He visited us on a whim, wanting to rekindle a relationship with Mom.

I followed him to the plastic-covered ivory couch and sat on his lap. "Aurorita, do you want a dollar?" he asked, as he removed one from his wallet.

"No, I want a five," I replied.

He smiled as he put the dollar bill back in his wallet and handed me a larger one.

Leaping off his lap, I squealed with delight. "I want to go to the *bodega*."

"Okay. Let's see if your brother and sister want to go."

Soon enough, the four of us were walking to Kino's, the local grocery store, with my hand in his. Even if it had been a scorching day with kids playing in the gushing open hydrant or the whimsical Mr. Softee truck dispersing free ice cream, I wouldn't have let go of my dad's warm hand.

At Kino's, I picked out assorted chips, bringing them eagerly to the register. "That's my family's dinner," I said, handing over the five dollars, excited to carry the paper bag home.

There, Mom asked Pancho to follow her into the kitchen, and about fifteen minutes later, without any preface, we were exchanging good-byes.

Tears welled up in my eyes when my arms wrapped around his neck. The apartment felt smaller once the door closed behind him. The dad I had wished for was gone as fast as he had come.

It wasn't until we were older that Mom shared the truth about Pancho's controlling, abusive, and unfaithful ways—characteristics that luckily I hadn't inherited. Regardless, hearing about his negative traits didn't quash my desire to meet him.

That spring, in Pancho's modest Los Angeles home, he seemed feeble, yet his presence exuded confidence. I smiled with genuine curiosity at the man who had helped give me life. We had the same olive complexion, oval face, high cheekbones, long nose, and small mouth, but it was odd seeing my biological father and not feeling any allegiance to him.

His first words when he saw me were, "Oh, my. . .you look just like your mother." He must've forgotten the tears he'd cried when he first carried me. Seeing his mirror image had filled him with remorse for having denied that I was his child during Mom's pregnancy.

My dad and I barely spoke during my stay. He remained in his bedroom for the majority of the time, leaving me to surmise that he preferred solitude. Respecting his privacy, I spent time with the rest of the family.

On the day of my departure, I said, "Pancho, I'm glad that I finally met you."

"Me too, Aurorita," he replied, using my middle name with much familiarity, "and I'm glad you got to meet the kids. Forgive me that we couldn't talk, but I needed to rest."

"It's okay." I kissed his cheek and hugged him.

My dad's detachment had been disappointing, though not surprising, but I was content that he was no longer an enigma.

I saw Pancho again in November 1996 while on a business trip. His wife answered the door and led me to the kitchen where my father suddenly said, "Aurorita, your mother was a difficult woman."

"You're crazy. My mom's a softy. You're the one that's not easy."

His wife made a hidden gesture suggesting his mind wasn't clear and then changed the subject. "Do you know you have two sisters in Cuba: Carmen's daughters, Teresa and Ileana?"

"I thought we were all here."

She handed me a sheet of paper. "Here's their address in Havana."

"Okay, thanks. . .I gotta go. I have a long day tomorrow." Little did I know that I would meet my sisters in the near future.

It was the last time I saw my father. He died in 2003 of natural causes at the age of eighty-six.

# *12*

# Original Bad Ass

LIFE IN THE REAL WORLD suddenly became scary when I graduated from my safe haven. Wanting a smooth transition from university life to full-time employment, I remained in New Brunswick and found a portraiture job.

Six months later, I began repaying student loans and realized that the chances of finding work as a fashion photographer were slim. A college degree, however, does not confine you to one area of study; it reveals other possibilities.

In the fall of 1989, the wheels of my future career began to spin during a reserve drill. An army staff sergeant, who was a narcotics investigator in his civilian job, stopped me one afternoon as I walked past his office.

"Specialist Torres, the Middlesex County Prosecutor's Office is hiring college graduates for investigators' positions. I think you'd be an ideal candidate. Why don't you send them your resume?"

"What would I be doing, Sergeant?"

"Investigating crimes committed in the county."

"That sounds cool. I'll think about it. Thank you, Sergeant."

Law enforcement was not a field I had considered, but I weighed his suggestion. Finding it to be a better job opportunity, I submitted my resume and was soon called for an interview.

That morning, I entered the vast gray-and-black-marble lobby of a tall glass building in downtown New Brunswick and made my way to the chief's office. A few moments later, I was asked to enter a spacious office where framed accolades adorned the walls and an American flag stood in the corner.

Three men rose to introduce themselves.

"Good morning Miss Torres. I'm Chief Dudas. This is Deputy Chief Bellagio and Assistant Prosecutor Fornoff. Please have a seat," said the Eastern European chief as he motioned to a chair in front of his desk.

Bellagio, a handsome Italian in his late forties, and Fornoff, a thin, red-faced Irishman about fifty-five years old, with more salt than pepper in his hair, followed suit.

After some small talk, the chief, who clearly controlled the room and was accustomed to others following his lead, got right to the point.

"Miss Torres, we have reviewed your resume along with those of many others. Your military experience, bachelor's degree, and fluency in Spanish are favorable. You have indicated that you are interested in an investigator's position. However, in order to be considered for that position, you must have previous law enforcement experience or three years as a prosecutor's agent in this office. Being that you have neither, we are prepared to offer you a position as a prosecutor's agent for the grand jury unit. Should you decide to accept it, your yearly salary will be $16,000, and you may begin within two weeks."

"What does that position entail, and what benefits does it include?" I inquired.

"Of course. Fair questions." He signaled to the assistant prosecutor. "He will answer your first question."

Fornoff began speaking matter-of-factly. "The position entails working for assistant prosecutors and preparing cases for the grand jury. This is a very busy office. The APs rely heavily on the agents' knowledge, expediency, and communication skills to ensure a case is presented appropriately in order to secure indictments. Agents gather evidence, interview victims, witnesses, and law enforcement, obtain further case information, and such." He nodded succinctly and looked at the deputy chief.

Speaking in a low voice, Bellagio answered the second question. "The benefits are good medical insurance, two weeks paid vacation, and holidays."

The chief took over without missing a beat. "Personnel can provide you with all the additional information you need."

It appeared the interview had ended. As they spoke, I had concluded that, although it was not the position I sought and the pay was lousy, it was an interesting career switch. "Okay, I'll take the job."

"Congratulations, Miss Torres." The chief rose and extended his hand to me; the others followed.

I left content with the fact that my future had taken a turn for the better.

READING THROUGH FILES TAUGHT ME much about the law; I

found it especially exciting when reading narcotics cases. Whenever undercover officers visited my office in preparation for their grand jury testimony, their stories held me captive. Their cases spun from a movie reel containing close calls and death-defying wit. The more we spoke, the more fascinated I became. I wanted to be part of that elite team whose responses to questions of being discovered, or in other scary situations, seemed too casual. "Yeah, but you gotta stay cool," or "No, I might be dead today."

At that time, a white guy with a ponytail and a diamond earring practically defined an undercover cop, but the Narcotics Task Force had an exceptional Puerto Rican operative in her mid-twenties named Mimi Alvarez. She worked a large number of the drug cases and had been able to infiltrate untouched places at a time when bilingual Hispanic women were a unique find in law enforcement—let alone undercover cases.

As I read her reports, I found myself wanting to do what she did. I couldn't wait to meet her. The first time I saw her in the office hallway, I stopped what I was doing and stood by my door, taking in her appearance: raggedy jeans, a light jacket wrapped around her waist, baggy crew-neck t-shirt, and long disheveled hair underneath a baseball cap.

*Wow, how cool is that! She looks normal.* I suddenly became the little girl who sees her hero for the first time. "Psst, Mimi?" I called out.

She turned, rolled police reports in her hand, and smiled. "Yeah. I'm Mimi."

"I'm Julia. Can you come into my office when you're done?"

"Right now good?"

"Yeah, of course."

She followed me into the square room that seemed to have expanded with her presence, and sat on the simple cloth-covered chair next to my metal filing cabinet. Clearing my desk, which became routine whenever she visited, I bombarded her with questions. "Tell me what you do. I think it's awesome. Tell me, tell me."

Mimi laughed. "Aw, that's sweet. What do you wanna know?"

"What's it like to be an undercover? How's it feel?"

"It's cool, different, uh—I don't know. It's just a job, you know." She shrugged.

I looked at her, baffled. "No, it's not just a job. Everybody doesn't do it, and not everyone can. I mean, when you're doing undercover work, are you thinking you're Mimi, or are you thinking you're the person you're pretending to be?"

"If I have to be aware of something Mimi needs to know, I'm Mimi. If I'm pretending to be the perp, then I'm the bad guy."

Juggling dual personalities without losing yourself, clever—you need innate skills for that, I thought.

"Did someone you know ever see you doing undercover, and if so, what'd you say?"

"No, that hasn't happened, but I'll tell you what did. One day I'm at the supermarket with my husband and kid—"

"Wait a minute. You have a husband and kid? What do they say about your job?"

"Oh, yeah. My husband doesn't like it. You know, he's got that Latino *machismo* thing going. My son's too little to say anything. He's two."

"Yeah, I know what you mean about the *machismo* thing.

I've met plenty of those." I rolled my eyes.

"Well, we were at the register, and I hear a guy behind me saying, 'Maria, *psst*, Maria.' That's my street name, and I'm not turning around, you know, cause I'm not Maria. But he continues, and I get curious to see who it is, so I turn around and see a target and play it off and say, 'Oh, shit, B. I didn't know it was you. I kept hearing my name, and I'm like, who the fuck can it be, and when I turn around, it's you.'"

"So what'd he say?"

"He thought I didn't want to speak to him 'cause I was with my family, but I said, 'Nah, I just wasn't paying attention.'"

"What'd your husband say?"

"Nothing. He knows not to say anything at a time like that."

"Well, that's good."

"Yeah. So you like this stuff, huh?"

"Yeah, I wanna do it."

"I see that. You're ready, huh?"

"Been ready."

"I could see you're hungry. You'd be good."

"Thanks. I am hungry."

"You just have to take it in stride."

"What do you mean?"

"You know, don't forget who you are, don't marry the job, find a way to de-stress. . .that kind of stuff."

Without a doubt, Mimi was the type of undercover cop I wanted to be. She introduced me to a world of danger, mayhem, and unparalleled excitement! There I was fresh out of college, wanting adventure, and Mimi spoke of things I could envision myself doing. I knew it was the next direction I'd pursue.

By then, I had been employed about six months and was

confident that I had acquired the investigative skills required to take my career one step further. With that intention, I wrote the chief a memo. His response left much to be desired—agents had to hold their position for three years. Having seen that was not always the case, I knew it would only be a matter of time before I went elsewhere.

A FEW WEEKS LATER, I left for my two-week annual army reserve training at Fort Indiantown Gap, Pennsylvania, to attend the Professional Leadership Development Course. It consisted of developing essential leadership skills and having military instructors grade your potential to lead.

One day in my platoon, Corporal Brennan, a twenty-year-old, prematurely gray Special Forces soldier, was chosen by our head M/I, to conduct a mock reconnaissance and told to select two soldiers from our platoon to complete the mission. The first soldier he chose was Reston, the platoon leader; the second was me. I knew I had to demonstrate my fullest potential just as I'd been doing in PT runs with Rangers and Special Forces soldiers.

Brennan, whom I highly respected and admired because of his leadership and specialized skills, felt I was capable of completing the task. Since Special Forces soldiers are taught not to make mistakes, he had to be right.

The M/I gave us an objective. "Here are your coordinates."

We removed all-weather maps from our cargo pockets.

"Go and report back on any terrain, weather, inhabitants, structures, food, and weapons. Seize items you deem essential, note their condition, and time and place they were found. If you are seen, heard, or captured, you fail. You have fifteen minutes. Go!"

After agreeing on a signal to regroup, off we went separately, moving with the stealth and swiftness familiar to soldiers who are well trained and enjoy what they do.

Surrounded by large trees and heavy foliage, I continued my trek leaping over rocks and ducking under branches until I reached my search point. I stopped, crouched behind a tree trunk for cover, and listened—nothing but the occasional bird tweet or bee buzz.

Slowly I rose, scanning the terrain for anything out of the ordinary, before moving with controlled speed until something to my far right caught my eye—a reflection of light. Finding no signs of entrapment, I moved forward, low to the ground, until I got to the target area. Sticking out at the bottom of a pile of rocks was a Ziploc bag containing a bit of hardened sand. I tugged at it and withdrew a weathered map with coordinates.

Then I heard Brennan's pre-arranged whistle. After noting pertinent data and securing the seized item in my cargo pocket, I moved rapidly to meet the team.

We advised the M/I of our discoveries and provided our seizures. He was astonished at one particular item—the long lost map I had found. Shaking his head in genuine surprise, he declared that previous classes hadn't found it. It made me proud that I hadn't let Brennan down.

On graduation day a few days later, I was elated to rise to my name and title of honor graduate. Because of it, I was placed on the commandant's list and invited to return as a military instructor for a six-month tour. I knew that I'd follow through with it, but when I returned to Middlesex, God had other plans.

*Bruno Bustamante, me, and Miguel Muñoz, June 1981, 8th Grade Graduation*

*Rudy Miret, June 1980, his 8th Grade Graduation*

*Emerson High School graduation with Lola, June 1985*

*Our only family portrait—Frank, Mom, me, and Marlene, 1984*

*Cecille Pagarigan and me, 1983, compliments of Caroline Wentworth*

*Before leaving Cuba, April 1970. I'm in the middle of the front row, to the right of my sister. My brother is second from the left, second row.*

*Our first winter in New Jersey, December 1970*

*Abuela and me, my 14th birthday party, April 1981*

*My grandfather, Celio Fundora Rosales, 1946*

*Tio Ramon, 1964*

*Pancho, 1951*

*Victory Tower, Fort Jackson, South Carolina, 1986*

*Mom, me, and Marlene, August 1986, a day before my graduation from Basic*

*Basic Training, Fort Jackson, South Carolina*

*Burns giving tactical pointers in barracks, December 1990*

*In a Langley Air Force Base hangar, January 1991*

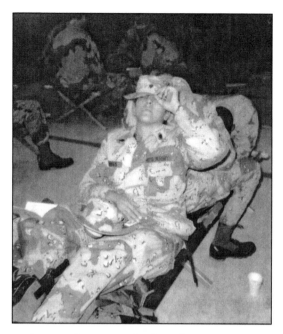

*Awaiting departure to Saudi Arabia, January 1991*

*On a mission with Burns, January 1991*

*Standing in front of my rig, January 1991*

*Sandstorm*

*Playing with knives in our hootch after a sandstorm, February 1991*

*Day of Cease Fire—One of the biggest missions in US history, February 1991*

*Buddy and me, in a picture taken by Lopez just after we heard of the Cease Fire.*

*Ross, me, and Lopez in our motor pool, March 1991*

*Playing Spades in our tent, March 1991*

*Trost getting ready to fuel up our rig, April 1991*

*Driving a rig on a mission with Trost, April 1991*

*Ross on shit detail, near the showers and latrines, May 1991*

*Soldier stirring the shit, May 1991*

*Me and my brother Ross, May 1991*

*With Manning at a Saudi taxi driver's house, June 1991*

*Loading APCs for redeployment, June 1991*

*One of the mechanics enjoying our makeshift pool, June 1991*

*With Mom on my return to Langley AFB, July 1991*

*At Langley, with Mom, Lopez, and Ross*

*Bible we were given in the desert*

*Desert Storm cassettes*

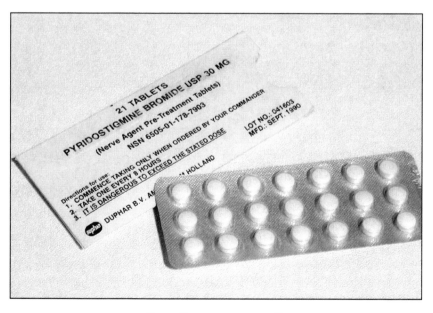

*Desert Storm nerve agent pills*

i spent extensive time working on this case just prior to the unit
redeployment the end of June.
I interviewed the Company Commander ███████████ the XO ██████████
████ 1SG ███████ as well as 37 other members of her unit to include
all PLT Sergeants and PLT Leaders. While in the beginning phases of the
inquiry I discovered that the 185th Trans Battalion, which the 424th TC was
part off, had an acting IG named MAJ ██████████ who was also the battalion XO.
No detailed IG in SWA new this. The 185th is a Cal NG unit and Maj ███████
is dully appointed by the state TAG. SPC Torres had taken her complaints to
MAJ ████████ before her mother ever got involved. ████████████████████████

████████████████████████████████████████████ I tried to interview MAJ
████████████ as well as the Battalion Commander LTC Chambers. I made several
appointments with them and when I showed up they were not there. This was
compounded when I discovered that the battalion had a policy that for a
soldier to go to the IG, Chaplain, or even to higher chain of command that
they must personally go to everyone in their chain of command and ask
permission, state their problem and give the people they were talking to the
opportunity to fix their problem. If the soldier wanted to go to the IG etc
directly they were not allowed to. Although I was unable to talk to the
Battalion Commander/XO about this I was able to verify this policy with 3
company commanders and the battalion S-1. Since the CMDR/XO successfully
evaded me until their redeployment I went to the 32d Trans Group Commander
COL Gaw about the 185th and it's polices and procedures. He basically said
that the 185th was a NG unit and had its own rules. As I said the 185th is a
California NG unit but the 424th Trans is a USAR unit out of Galax, Virginia.
This is background information and sets the tone for the problems Torres was
having in her unit. She wasn't getting anywhere with getting then resolved.
Torres's complaints basically boil down to harassment. ████████████████████
████████████████████████████████████████████████████████. I think they
████████████████████████████████████████ None of the chain of command
have any complaints about her work. ████████████
████████████████████████████████. She denies any harassment by her superiors. It seems
to be that some of the soldiers in the unit came on to her and were put down.
Those same soldiers then took to harassing her. SGT Torres had a group of
soldiers that she was friends with and she tried to spend time with them. The
entire chain of command talked during the interviews about hearing rumors
about what was going on but they couldn't act on rumors. I informed them that
was an entirely wrong answer. ████████████████████████████

████████████████████████████████████████████████████

*Follow up thru NGB*
*on this.*

*Redacted minutes, sexual harassment investigation (page 1)*

---

████ ██████████. This is one of the items that . Torres brought up to
Maj ████████.
SGT Torres was harassed by her peers but not her superiors. Her superiors
instead of helping her solve her problems, hindered her. ████████████████████
████████████████████████████████████████

UPDATE
The 80th Training Division IG, LTC Gentile, is also looking into the systemic
problems in the 424. He is going out to the unit the end of August to do a
sensing session.

*Redacted minutes, sexual harassment investigation (page 2)*

06 JUN 91 (QUANDER)

Received another congressional request for information on behalf of a Senator. Letter written by a former CW# now a civilian pilot. Sent reply out to MC with CF to OCLL ref # 1051938. CASE CONT.

19 JUL 91 (QUANDER)

Reviewed this case, after call to SWA must send out an interim ltr informing MC of additional time required. Interim response out on 19 Jul 91, to MC with CF to OCLL ref # 1051938. CASE CONT.

15 OCT 91 (QUANDER)

Long overdue, this response was one of three I had that was lost in the mail from SWA to DAIG. Any way, the allegation of harassment by fellow soldiers (peers) in her unit against SP4 Torres was substantiated. ███████████████████████████████████ The Acting IG was the Bn XO. Acting IG and Bn Cdr basically ignored not only Torres pleas for help but the IGs' attempts to speak with them concerning their lack of concern. There was no harassment against Torres by her superiors although they did nothing to assist her. ████████ ████████████████ Torres was a city soldier from New Jersey assigned to a unit from rural Virginia. Her attempts to be friendly were mistaken as come ons by some of her peers. Not so. ████████████████████████ ███████████████████████ It was to late. No one was able to help SP4 Torres until her mother wrote to Senator Robb and the case was referred to DAIG for action. The case was forwarded to ARCENT-IG and they became actively involved with the problem. Botton line. Allegation was ████████████ Appropriate action has been initiated with NGB and Fifth Army-IG. ███████████████████████████ Final response out to three MCs with CF to OCLL ref # 1051938, 1091214, and 1043460. CF to First Army-IG and to Fifth Army-IG on or about 16 Oct 91. CASE CLOSED.

*Redacted minutes, sexual harassment investigation (page 3)*

OFFICE OF THE ASSISTANT SECRETARY OF DEFENSE
1200 DEFENSE PENTAGON
WASHINGTON, DC 20301-1200

SEP 2 7 2005

Julia Torres                    20894[000
2150 Oakmont Dr
Flowers Ranch Fl 33603-1833

Dear Julia Torres:

We in the Department of Defense care very much about the health of those now serving and of those who have previously served. Some years ago we contacted Gulf War veterans of units that were near Khamisiyah, Iraq, between March 10 and March 13, 1991, to inform them of possible exposure to very low levels of chemical warfare agents released during demolition operations following the war. We are now contacting you again because there is some new information that may interest you.

In the August issue of the *American Journal of Public Health*, Institute of Medicine researchers compared the causes of death and their rates among U.S. Army Gulf War veterans whose units might have been exposed to very low levels of chemical warfare agents with U.S. Army Gulf War veterans whose units were unlikely to have been exposed. The rates and causes of death for both groups were similar. The overall rate of death for cancer was the same, with only a slightly higher death rate due to brain cancer among servicemembers assigned to units that might have been exposed.

The results of this study were based on death records from 1991 through 2000. The Department of Veterans Affairs (VA) is continuing to conduct death rate studies of all Gulf War veterans. These results should help to clarify the long-term health outcomes of Gulf War veterans, including those linked to the Khamisiyah demolition. We will continue to monitor findings for any indication of specific health-related issues.

We have enclosed a fact sheet and answers to frequently asked questions to provide you with more detailed information about this recent study.

Your health is important to you and to us, and if you have health concerns, problems or questions, you should consult with your primary care physician. Both the DoD and the VA offer medical evaluation programs for Gulf War veterans. To schedule an appointment, call toll-free at 1-800-796-9699 for the DoD program or 1-800-749-8387 for the VA program. For general information about Khamisiyah and related issues, please call 1-800-497-6261.

Sincerely,

Ellen P. Embrey
Deputy Assistant Secretary of Defense
Force Health Protection and Readiness

Enclosure

*Gulf War Veterans letter*

# *13*

# The Known and Unknown War

O NE COOL SEPTEMBER AFTERNOON in 1990, my contribution to world history began to emerge. First Sergeant Collins made an announcement to our reserve unit. "Company, at ease! As you know, Saddam Hussein invaded Kuwait last month."

You could hear a pin drop.

"Volunteers are being requested—"

*I'm going.*

"—for Operation Desert Shield. If anyone would like their name placed on the list, please see me after formation. Attention! Fall out!"

Amid murmurs and shuffling, everyone in the unit dispersed, except me.

We were not a combat unit, but combat support; our job was to provide training for troops.

Our company had a good command structure, honorable leaders who'd stand for what was right despite opposition. Because of that, our unit was cohesive and ran smoothly.

I approached Collins. "Top, put my name on the list."

Transportation was a slot I'd be filling, perhaps replacing someone unprepared to go. At the same time, I wondered if I'd have the opportunity to be in combat again. In hindsight, my thoughts, noble or not, were secondary. Subconsciously, I was daring fate to take my life.

ONE EARLY EVENING the third week of November at Mom's house, I was lying on the futon in my old room, reading Truman Capote's In Cold Blood, when the telephone interrupted.

"Specialist Torres?" Top's clear, scratchy voice could only have one purpose.

"Yes, First Sergeant."

"Your orders are in."

"Okay, Top. Where am I going?"

"Fort Eustis, Virginia. You're assigned to the 4-2-4 Transportation Company, a reserve unit from Galax, Virginia. They are waiting to be shipped out to Saudi Arabia."

"When do I leave, First Sergeant?"

"The twenty-seventh. . .we worked it out so you'd be home for Thanksgiving. You'll be gone a minimum of 180 days. Call your job, let them know you don't know when you'll be back, and that your employment is protected under the Soldiers and Sailors Relief Act. Lieutenant Perez is squaring away your travel. He'll drop off your plane ticket and your orders on his way home."

"Yes, Top. And thanks for Thanksgiving. I know my

mom will appreciate it."

"You're welcome. Take all your military gear. If you're missing something, you'll get it over there. Let us know if you need anything while you're overseas. Someone from the unit will stay in touch. Good luck, Specialist Torres. I know you'll do well."

"Thank you, First Sergeant."

I hung up the phone. *Wow, I'm going to war.*

There was no doubt in my mind that matters would escalate and I'd be part of a historical event, just as I'd always wanted. I was not afraid but excited, prepared mentally and physically to assume leadership if or when required.

Dying was not a deterrent. What would I lose, my life? I didn't care; I felt it had already been lost. If I died, at least I'd die honorably, doing something I loved. In addition, and on a much larger scale, I'd finally find peace.

As I moved quickly to prepare two duffel bags, the corridor door clicked open. Mom's footsteps echoed until she stopped at our front entrance. Keys jingling, she saw my room light on and shouted, "Yoo-hoo!"

"I'm here," I answered. After leaning my cargo against the wall, I headed to the kitchen to relay the unexpected news. "Hi, Ma. How was work?" I asked, kissing her on the cheek.

She put her purse on the table. "Busy. I'm beat."

"Want me to make you espresso?"

"No, I just need to sit for a few minutes. What are you doing?"

"Not much. Ma, I gotta tell you something."

Her eyebrows furrowed. "What happened?"

"Nothing happened, Ma. My sergeant called me."

"From the army?"

"Yeah."

"What for?"

"To tell me my orders came in."

"What orders? What are you talking about, Aurorita?"

There was no simple way to inform her. "I'm going to Virginia. Then I'm going to Saudi Arabia."

The lines on her forehead deepened. She covered her mouth in horror, eyes filling with tears.

"Ma, stop. Nothing's gonna happen."

"Who else is going?"

"Nobody."

"What do you mean, *nobody?* All those men, and none of them are going?"

"They need truck drivers. I'll be going with other people." Certain that she wouldn't have understood, I hadn't told her I'd volunteered.

"But why? You're a woman. That's for men," she argued.

"Ma, it's not just for men," I said, shaking my head.

"Aurorita, you're going to *war!*" she added, frantically.

"I know. I want to go."

"I don't understand you. Who in their right mind wants to go to *war?*"

"I do. I'm not afraid."

She scoffed, "I *know* that. Maybe you *should* be. You could die!"

"Ma, we can all die at any moment."

"It's not the same to come across a den of lions as it is to go inside it on purpose."

"I'm going. I already started packing."

"Already? When are you leaving?"

"Tuesday."

"That's *soon*." She started to cry.

"Don't cry, Ma." I kissed her forehead and gave her a firm hug. "Don't worry. I'm gonna be fine. At least I'll be here for Thanksgiving."

ON THE EARLY MORNING AIRPLANE RIDE to Fort Eustis, my mind entertained thoughts on what the unit members would be like. Since I was an outsider, I hoped they'd be accepting.

Once I landed, a cabbie dropped me off at the barracks where I climbed out wearing jeans, sneakers, and a sweatshirt, carrying a full duffel bag in front and another in back. The unit was in formation.

As I walked up the barracks steps, I felt eyes behind me; I turned. Most of the soldiers were staring at me. In that moment, I sensed I'd have problems with that unit.

After returning their stare, I marched down the long, buffed hallway where a standing metal fan was blowing. At the first sergeant's office, I tapped twice, entered the small, ordinary room and stood before him. His name tag read *Fifer*. "First Sergeant, Specialist Torres reporting for duty."

Seated on a cushioned chair behind a metal desk, a wad of chewing tobacco pooled under his bottom lip, Fifer, head tilted to the left, sized me up. Sweeping his hand forward, in a deep Southern accent, he said, "Sit."

After lining up each duffel bag neatly in front of me, I sat gazing blankly at the silent black-and-white clock above his head. When he did not address me, I removed the orders from my denim pocket and extended them. "Specialist Torres reporting for duty, First Sergeant," I repeated.

My arm remained out while he looked at me in contemplation—hand curled, bent index finger over mouth, eyes ticking in rapid succession.

"Should I change into my uniform, First Sergeant?" I asked, feeling like a mind reader.

The chair screeched as he rolled forward in it. *"That'd* be a good *i*-de-a," he replied in a sneering drawl.

I knew I was not welcome.

A few hours later during the company's next formation of 181 soldiers—12 women and 169 men, I looked around my platoon for the biggest guy, convinced that I'd have to have a best friend who would stick with me through thick or thin, just as I would with him.

That's when I found Burns. He was a sergeant and the leader of third squad; I had been placed in second. At first impression, he appeared to be the type of person who'd stand up for someone who was mistreated; I hoped I wasn't wrong.

Since neither size nor strength equated with integrity, that week I began to watch him discreetly to assess his character. Higher ranks respected Burns, often designating him to leadership positions, which he handled with fairness and responsibility. Disagreeing with a troop meant he'd make his point clear, without intimidation.

Although he remained alone most of the time, he wasn't introverted or biased, speaking to everyone in the same respectful fashion. My decision was made—whether he liked it or not, he'd be my best friend.

At the end of our last formation that Friday, I turned to him, hand extended. "How you doin', Burns? I'm Torres.

You're gonna be my best friend."

He chuckled but did not shake my hand.

"Don't leave me hanging. Shake my fuckin' hand," I ordered.

Burns became serious and squinted, searching my eyes.

"O-kay," he said, slowly shaking the tips of my fingers.

I nodded and marched away.

Every day thereafter, I'd make it a point to challenge him to a fight whenever I saw him teaching other soldiers defensive tactics. I figured that he'd eventually get curious to know my angle and speak to me. I believed he'd concede to being my best friend when he discovered our similar mindsets.

The next weekend in the barracks first-floor day room, soldiers in civvies were playing pool while Burns sat on a couch, watching television. Standing by the sofa, two bags of chips in one hand, soda in the other, I asked, "Hey, Burns, whatcha' doing over here all by your lonesome self?"

He glanced my way. "Watching TV."

Shouts of soldiers at the pool table made it hard to hear. "Doesn't the yelling bother you?"

"No, uh-uh."

"You tune it out?"

"Yup." His head ping-ponged between the television and me.

"You want one?" I offered a bag of chips and sat next to him.

"No, thank you."

He's still watching TV, I thought. "You sure?" I asked before opening one. "They sure are good. You know, when I was a kid and went to parties, chips were my thing. Forget the ice cream. Forget the cake. I'd stuff my face by the chips table—it didn't matter what they were, but I loved the cheese doodles best."

My silly monologue had finally stirred him. "Why was that the best?"

"Are you kidding? Sucking my fingers was like dessert."

He snorted, and so did I.

"You're a trip," he said, shaking his head and smiling.

"Ah, got you interested, but I don't know about all that. I'm just me. You don't say much, huh?"

"No."

"Why not? I don't bite and if you're thirsty, I'll even let you have some of my soda." I said, extending it out to him, before adding, "I don't have any communicable diseases, you know. No cooties over here."

He shook his hand, declining the soda, and laughed. "I'm sure you don't have any whatchacall cooties. I just like to stay to myself."

I nodded before saying, "I gotta tell you something. I was watching you."

He let out a hearty shout. "Good Lord! Watching me for what?"

"To see if you were good enough to be my best friend."

His forehead wrinkled. "Good enough to be your best friend?"

"Yeah. That's what you're gonna be, you know."

"You sure, huh?"

"Yup, just like you say."

He laughed. "Torres, can I ask you something?"

"Sure."

"Why you so bold? Ain't nobody ever spoken to me like that before."

"Like what?"

"Like the first time you took your hand out."

"Oh, that. I don't think of myself as bold. I just say what I mean."

"Say what you mean, is that what you call it? I asked myself, 'Who is this nervy, self-confident female?' You sure do speak with authority. It scares people."

"You scared?" I teased before taking a swig of my soda.

"No, uh-uh, not me. But a whole lot of these men are."

I shrugged. "That's their problem. I figured you thought I was nuts."

"Well, yeah," he snickered. "But then I saw that look in your eyes."

"What look?"

"That cut-your-heart-out-look."

"Get outta here!" I chuckled, slapping his arm. "Well, don't worry—I've never cut anybody's heart out."

"Not yet. . .I admire your boldness. I said to myself, 'Goodness gracious, who is this little lady speaking to me like that?'"

"You said that already."

"Well, yes, but I'm a trooper for the North Carolina Highway Patrol. I ain't never heard someone come across that way."

"You act as if I'm a rare breed. Come to Jersey. It's one of those rare places that you get respect for saying the truth."

"Is everybody there like that?"

"I'd have to say yes, for the most part."

"Oh. Good gosh. The women, too?"

"Uh, yeah, that would be everybody," I answered, shaking my head and raising my eyebrows.

"They all look like you, too?"

"You mean with two eyes, two ears, a nose, and mouth?" He looked down with a sheepish grin. "Where you from?"

"You mean my background?"

"Yes."

"I'm Cuban."

"Really? I'm part Cuban, too."

"Oh, yeah? Cool. I've got other parts, too. What are yours?"

"Part African-American, and part Seminole Indian."

"Oh, that's where you get that reddish-brown hue. That's awesome. I haven't met any Native Americans in Jersey. I'm honored to meet a real American."

"Real American?"

In between crunching on my second bag of chips, I added, "Yeah, you were here before anybody else arrived. We're all immigrants you know, except the Indians. Most people seem to forget that."

"Hm. You're right."

"I know. I don't speak if I'm wrong."

"Is that right?"

"Yes."

"So what are your other parts?"

"My mom's side comes from the Canary Islands, France, and Scotland. My dad's side has Italian, Native Cuban-Indian, and also the Canary Islands."

"That's a whole lot."

"That's why I say I'm Cuban. You know, the KISS method, Keep It Simple, Stupid. If I say all that, people begin to look at me like this." I brought my face close to his and squinted, head tilted in exaggeration. "Makes me feel like a Martian."

"Like that, huh," he said, cracking up. "Well, you're not common in these parts, and they don't get out much. Some of these men haven't even been out of the county, never mind another state like New York. Good gosh, they'd say that's where the Yankees are from. They don't like them Yankees."

I rolled my eyes. "That's ridiculous."

"So tell me, what do you think about the troops?"

"Some are nice, others treat me with indifference, and many are immature. Burns, I don't put up with juvenile behavior in adults."

"Me neither."

"Of course not, you're a cop. I'm in law enforcement, too. I'll be going to the police academy when I return."

"That'd be good for you. You're quick on your feet and not afraid of facing people."

"Thank you."

"You're welcome."

"Well, buddy—is it okay if I call you buddy?"

"Well, is that what you *wanna* call me?"

"Yeah—I mean, well, what's your first name?"

"Lester."

"Yuck. You don't look like a Lester."

"Well, Torres, what does a Lester look like?"

"Not like you. What's your middle name?"

"Eugene."

"Man, they killed you both ways. What were your parents thinking? Nope, Buddy will have to do, or Burns. I don't wanna strip you of your identity."

He chortled. "What's your name?"

"Julia. You can call me Julia or Torres. I don't care which."

"Can I call you either one, or do I have to pick one?"

"Either." I yawned. "Well, Buddy, Burns, I'm going to bed. Glad you finally spoke to me—" I rose from the couch—"and didn't look at me like I was from another planet. Good-night."

"Well, you have a good-night, too."

At the door, Buddy called out, "Torres?"

"Yeah?"

"You're all right."

"I know," I smiled, tossing my trash in the garbage can.

That was the beginning of an invaluable friendship, one that some soldiers and the command could not understand. Together overseas, Burns and I would come across figurative land mines purposefully set out to destroy us.

# *14*

# Two Vipers, One Desert Fox, and a Dog

ITHIN A WEEK OF MY ARRIVAL, a few male soldiers had begun to sexually harass me with unwanted come-ons, specifically a twenty-year-old named Lyre. He lingered outside after formation early one evening.

Hands in his pockets, hat loose on his head, he strode towards me. "Say, Te-rez?" he called out, as I headed to the steps of the barracks front corner entrance.

Annoyed, I turned and asked, "What?"

His small beady eyes appeared uncertain. "Well, you're a good-looking woman. I'm a good-looking man."

I scoffed. "That's your opinion."

"How about me and you go make some babies?"

"Lyre, you're getting on my nerves," I said, standing in a

defensive posture—arms crossed, squared shoulders, feet shoulder-width apart. "What the fuck you talkin' about now?"

Removing his hands from his pockets, he used them to make a point. "Well, you're single, and I'm single. How about we get together and stop being single?"

"Lyre, I already told you more than once, I'm not interested."

"But how can you say that when you don't know me?"

"I don't need to know you."

He scratched his forehead, actually seeming dumbfounded. "Well, why not Te-rez?"

"You're not my type."

"And how do you know that?"

"Because I know what I like, and you're not it."

"But you—"

"Look, what don't you get? I don't fuckin' like you *now*, and I'm not gonna fuckin' like you *later*. If I did, I'd tell you, 'cause I'm not the shy type, so cut the bullshit."

I stormed off and entered the barracks, leaving him standing there with his mouth agape, a quizzical look on his face. I couldn't have been any clearer, yet he persisted.

After a few more instances of his inappropriate behavior, I decided to speak to someone in my chain of command, knowing the problem would escalate overseas if it wasn't addressed stateside.

The two principal leaders of a company are the first sergeant and the commanding officer. The first sergeant is in charge of the enlisted troops and is the principal assistant to the CO, who is in charge of the officers within the company and answers to the battalion commander.

The chain of command generally works as follows—if an enlisted soldier has an issue, he or she brings it to the squad leader's attention first. If it's not resolved, it continues up the COC to the platoon sergeant, then the first sergeant, who may take it to the sergeant major at the next level—battalion. Otherwise, the first sergeant, using his discretion, may turn to the executive officer and/or the commanding officer at the company level.

If nothing is done within the COC at the company level, the soldier then goes to the COC at the battalion level, where the chaplain and the inspector general are usually the next steps, and it may continue from there.

However, due to the lengthy time and aggravation it takes to continue up the COC at the company level, open-door policies may exist, allowing a soldier to speak directly to the first sergeant. It is a wise decision to have that policy in effect if an issue is followed up on, though the CO is ultimately responsible because he or she can correct the problem at its inception. Eventually, if no one does anything on any level, everyone is liable.

A few days later, I decided to speak with the first sergeant. Tapping twice on the outside of his open door, I stuck my head in, noticing his back to the entrance. "First Sergeant?"

The wheels of his chair squeaked when he swiveled in it. "Yes, Specialist Te-rez?"

"May I come in to speak with you? It's private."

His mouth stretched a tad, making me feel like I'd be a bother, but I wasn't deterred. I entered and continued, "If you don't mind, I'm gonna close the door, so nobody listens."

"Go ahead." He waved his hand dismissively.

Seated across from him, I began to explain the sexual harassment I had initially experienced, which had ceased, except
for Lyre. In his usual posture—head tilted to the side, fingers
of one hand curled near his mouth, the other hand on the arm-
rest—the first sergeant listened without interrupting.

"First Sergeant, I have a feeling this is gonna escalate
when we're overseas if it's not addressed here. Will you speak
to him and ask him to leave me alone?"

"Te-rez," he began, "you're a good-looking sol-jah." He
paused, interlocked his hands, placing them across his stomach, and leaned back in his chair. "You're gonna have these
problems." He stared at me impassively and didn't utter another word. Neither did I.

His answer had spoken volumes; I left his office having read
between the lines. His view, like that of others, was that I had
to pay the price for entering a man's world. Nothing would be
done in my defense; it'd be up to me to take care of it. The initial
hunch I had when I first arrived had been confirmed.

After chow that night, I saw Lyre walking down the hallway toward the day room. From across the hall I shouted,
mindless of anyone around. *"Lyre!"* I ambled across in battle
mode.

He turned. "Hey, Ter—"

"Wait!" I commanded.

He stood, curiously staring ahead until I was in front of
him.

"I'm gonna say this fuckin' shit once, and that's it, 'cause
I hate fuckin' repeating myself."

The creases on his forehead deepened.

"If you continue to bother me with your fuckin' bullshit,

you're gonna regret it. I'm not gonna put up with it, so you better stop the fuckin' shit right now!"

"Well, Te-rez, you don't have to get so upset about it."

"Yes, I do. I told you nicely a few times, but you didn't get it. Now I throw in more curses than last time, and you suddenly get it. What the fuck?"

"I'm sorry. I won't bother you again."

"Good. That's what you should've said the first time." I stomped away. We didn't have another problem, but that served as my preparation for the greater hurdles I'd have to jump overseas.

The days moved fast as we trained heavily; by the second week of December, I noticed a new guy standing at the end of the fourth squad in my platoon. He stuck out like a sore thumb—thick mustache, white skinny jeans, long-sleeved blue-and-white striped button-down shirt.

*Yay, he's Puerto Rican.* It was a relief not to be the only Hispanic. We glanced at each other; our eyes spoke of friendship, our smiles confirmed it—words were superfluous.

We approached one another after falling out. Smiling warmly with his soft brown eyes, he introduced himself. "Hi, Torres, I'm Lopez."

I could tell he was a man of strong convictions, who would not be influenced easily. I liked him already.

"Hi, Lopez, I'm glad you're here. Now I'm not the only Spanish person."

He smiled. "I understand. Where are you from?"

"I'm Cuban. Listen, I gotta tell you right away, don't be surprised if a guy named Kinney asks you if you speak Puerto Rican."

Laughing, showing a strong set of white teeth, he said, "He asked you if you spoke Cuban?"

"Yeah, and he asked if I ate beans and tacos, too."

Now we were both laughing.

"And another thing, Lopez."

"Oh-oh. What's that?"

"Believe it or not, he asked if I was black or white, cause I was dark but had straight hair."

"Torres, I can believe it. They're not used to seeing other people."

"See, that's a reason we have an edge growing up where we do. We get things quick and come across all kinds of people."

"Yes, that's right."

"So where in New York do you live?"

Smiling, he asked, "You know I'm from New York, huh?"

"Yeah, come on, where else? Look at your clothes."

His smile broadened. "I'm from Queens. You?"

"Jersey."

"When did you get here?"

"The twenty-seventh. You met Burns yet?"

"No. Who's that?"

"He's someone you'll be able to trust. Come on, I'll introduce you."

Lopez became the third link in the inner circle Burns and I had created.

Battle gear, with the exception of weaponry, was soon issued. Rifles would be issued prior to shipping out, but we would get our ammunition and grenades on the plane before we set foot in country.

ONE SUNDAY AFTERNOON, Burns, Lopez, and I were discussing buying radios for communication when a soldier named Ross overheard us and said, "I wanna go and buy one, too."

We looked at one another and agreed. The four of us purchased radios at the PX, giving each other code names: Burns and Lopez were Viper I and Viper II, Ross was Rossdog, and I was Desert Fox.

Ross, an African-American from Richmond, Virginia, whose family was from South Carolina, was the oldest and funniest soldier among us. He spoke "Geechee," a Creole language of the Gullah people, who live along the coast of South Carolina and Georgia. Geechee can be hard to decipher when you first hear it. Words like "leotard" are pronounced *le-a-taad*.

When he first approached me in the platoon, he asked, "E', Dyeréz, yeu wanna go PX wit meh?"

I replayed his question in my head, hearing two letters clearly. "No, thank you. I don't wanna go to the PX," I replied.

"A-ri." Raising his right shoulder, he strolled off with a slight swagger.

We enjoyed hanging out with him at the Non-Commissioned Officers Club because he was fun, endearing, and took most things in stride. His personality can be best illustrated by a phrase he often used: "I may be ole, but I ai't cole, sista." Ross was a loyal friend; I was honored to be the "sista" he confided in.

Typically, during our free times at night in Fort Eustis, we bowled or frequented a nightclub. On one of those nights, I became friends with Manning, a white female supply sergeant on orders from Fort Bragg, North Carolina. Sometimes, she'd join us at the club; it was a pleasure having another woman to speak with whose views paralleled mine.

We didn't know until many years later that Manning had ordered 181 body bags for our unit, including her own. A senior non-commissioned officer had told her that we were not expected to return alive; replacements had already been lined up, ready to be shipped out overseas within three months of our deployment.

On a Sunday afternoon, while Burns, Lopez, and I were discussing the unit's lack of Southern hospitality, I asked Burns, "Buddy, why are they like that?"

"Well, Torres, the senior NCOs feel the 'Yankees can't be trusted,' and that 'the women are gonna get us killed.'"

"But why?" I asked.

He shrugged. "I don't know. I told them you're all educated and have good ideas, but they don't want to listen."

"I'm not surprised," Lopez interjected.

"I guess they're still fighting the war between the North and the South," I said.

"Yup, that's it," Burns agreed.

"You should remind them who won."

The guys laughed.

Forewarned is forearmed, I thought.

With mobilization approaching, we moved into combat-ready roles when weapons were issued. The original figure of 181 soldiers dropped to 169, 11 women and 158 men, due to some of the soldiers' medical inability to travel overseas.

On our final free night at Fort Eustis, Burns, Lopez, and I enjoyed our time at the club, knowing it might be the last one we'd have under carefree conditions. Lopez and I shared a dance when the classic "Unchained Melody," by the Righteous Brothers, began playing.

Our slow steps and warm embrace seemed to say goodbye to the people we were: I wished the song would go on as the platonic love I felt coming from Lopez spilled into my core. The ambiguous life that we'd soon live filled the heavy air, so much that when the song ended we held hands and paused. The intensity in our eyes spoke of the unforeseen; in that single silent moment, time and space ceased.

Lopez leaned across, gently kissing me on the lips. The electrical current from his warm tap sealed our thoughts; we were ready for whatever came our way, having accepted the probability of either's death.

The three of us headed back to the barracks. In the brisk evening sky, three bright objects—the Orion, the North Star, and the moon—lit our path. Our steps were slow, but on either end, I could hear Burns and Lopez moving with controlled purpose. Entering the three-story brick building in silence, we parted for our quarters.

During lockdown the next and last night before deployment, I passed a room where six morose troops caught my eye. Stopping outside it, I asked, "What's up? Why the long faces?"

One replied, "We're just sitting here thinking that we don't know if we're all gonna make it back."

"No shit, Sherlock! You're thinking 'bout that now?"

There was silence.

"Our lives are not our own the minute we sign that paper. We belong to Uncle Sam." I paused at each one and said,

"You know, I'm better off than all of you. I volunteered for this war. I've already accepted the fact that I might die. You guys were ordered, and it still hasn't sunk in. That's a problem."

Staring at one specifically, I challenged, "And you wanna be a cop? You better think twice." I turned around and left.

Yes, I was fine with dying.

In retrospect, I could see why. Volunteering had been my choice. If I died, I'd own my death. I'd be the victor.

# 15

# In Country

D EPLOYMENT TO SAUDI ARABIA began in the wee hours of
January 5, 1991, after stripping our quarters and downing
OJ and oatmeal. We headed to an airplane hangar at Langley
Air Force Base in Virginia, where cameras rolled as reporters
spoke somberly into microphones.

The excited, nervous energy of hundreds of service members welcomed us as we marched to our designated waiting
area. Buddy and I sat back to back on a cot, playing Tetris and
solving crossword puzzles, respectively. In like manner,
Lopez, sitting next to us, listened to music through his headphones, drowning out the familiar *vroom* of F-14s overhead
while other soldiers played Spades and chewed gum or tobacco.
Seated next to him was Ross, the ever-present archivist who
had started a letter and put it away to remove a Polaroid cam-
era from his cargo pocket.

We smiled at the Instamatic—the soft, smooth zip of the emerging photograph capturing untainted faces huddled on a cot, rifles nearby. In our new desert camo uniforms, still fresh from our showers, we were the cleanest we'd look and smell for a long time.

Over the intercom a few hours later, our company was called. We secured our items, slung rifles on our shoulders, and marched in single file onto the commercial aircraft.

Our trek over thousands of miles began. Somewhere over the Atlantic Ocean, Sergeant Sara from Philadelphia, Pennsylvania, who was seated next to Sergeant Trost from Rochester, New York, got sick. Trost summoned a medic, who administered a sedative. All other eyes remained fixed on the movie—*Days of Thunder*.

Operation Desert Shield had the potential of escalating. The probability of combat in Iraq remained an unspoken certainty in the back of soldiers' minds. In lieu of anticipating what was coming, we enjoyed mundane activities as a welcome reprieve.

On the upper deck, scents of cinnamon-red gum filled the air, jokes were told, and boisterous card games ran rampant. In the lower deck, some soldiers listened to music through their cassette players; others played with Nintendo Gameboys in silence, undisturbed by the loud neighboring snores.

Many hours later, some who'd remained awake watched the sun rise over Monte Carlo; others fixed their sights on another movie—*Ghost*. Soon after, the mountains of Rome were an arresting sight when we stopped to refuel.

As our destination grew closer, a handful of soldiers stood up to take pictures of the Nile River in Egypt. Then, our lanky, thin-lipped executive officer, Lieutenant Pugh, came slowly down the aisle. "Troops—" he paused every few feet, placing his hand on the headrests and, through beady hazel eyes behind dark round prescription glasses, repeated, "Start getting ready."

A sudden shift in concentration followed. Headphones were removed, items stowed in overhead compartments. Noise from players in card games dropped a few notches as current hands were finished, changing the usual style of Spades from a thundering, friendly trumpet to a droning, syncopated drum. Sleeping soldiers were nudged, dreams extinguished by leaden words: "Wake up. We're almost there." A plethora of warped, murky images frazzled our awakened state as the unspoken tension thickened.

Outside the aircraft window, the darkness assumed a different feeling—ominous, abysmal. The nature of our operation was not in sync with the flight attendants' final call: *Is there anything else I can get for you?*

Dissociation began to manifest itself as doubts ran amok. Our mission meant emotion had to cease.

We arrived in country with the sound of a smooth halt on the tarmac of the King Fahd International Airport in Dammam. Troops let out deep sighs, closed their eyes, or entered into a hyper-vigilant state: eyes darting from side to side, jaws tight, breathing constrained.

Lined-up at the airplane door, immediate ammo—two forty-round magazines and two M67 grenades—were supplied. One magazine went in our weapon, the other in our cargo pocket or ammo pouch; the two grenades were hooked onto our bullet-resistant vests.

Weapons were locked and loaded—each announcing another soldier's entry into the unknown. In battle mode, we headed down the metal stairs into the dark, quiet, chilly desert, where stars twinkled magnificently in the sky, its beauty ill suited to our mood. The air was clear, easy to breathe in, but thoughts and voices were weighted, disheveled.

Some soldiers affirmed, "We're here."

Others questioned, "Are we really here?"

A few murmured in denial. "This isn't real."

The pessimist, the one you least wanted by your side, grumbled, "Am I coming home in a box?" or "Who's not gonna make it?"

The brutally honest were concise—"Shit, this is fucked up," while the goal-oriented said, "Let's do it." My sentiments included the first and last.

Orders came in whispers. "Go straight to those buses." Although there were many of us, our footsteps did not echo. With our protective masks strapped around our thighs, Kevlar helmets on our heads, and body armor on our chests, we boarded at sling arms.

Cruising down the barren road to Khobar Towers, where Arabic signs read from right to left, we stopped at pre-arranged checkpoints.

Units had been in the Gulf since August 1990, when President Saddam Hussein invaded Kuwait with Iraqi forces. His invasion, presumed to be a bluff until he ordered it, had surprised most of the world. In an attempt to seize Kuwaiti oil fields, his forces had occupied downtown Kuwait City and were en route to the Saudi Arabian border.

News of the attack had instantly reached Washington,

D.C., and the largest mobilization of American forces since the Vietnam War had followed in support of Operation Desert Shield. In no time, members of the 82$^{nd}$ Airborne Division and three hundred combat aircraft had been deployed to Saudi Arabia. Within a few months, hundreds of thousands would follow.

American commanders had considered the initial plan to drive Iraqi forces from Kuwait too much of a risk, resulting in an increase of troops deployed. Reinforcement came from coalition forces: Kuwait, the United Kingdom, Saudi Arabia, France, Canada, Egypt, Syria, Qatar, and the United Arab Emirates. The United Nations and twenty-three other countries also supported America.

At Khobar, we found spots for ourselves as instructed. Soon thereafter, Captain Huff, the commanding officer, began to demonstrate inconsistent leadership.

He ordered the eleven women to relocate to the ground floor to prevent interaction between the sexes. Amid our groans and grumbling, he continued, "If you think you're being segregated, it's because you are, and if you bitches have something to bitch about, bitch now."

That led to his next unnecessary decision: Everyone had to be in full uniform daily, even when smoking on the balcony.

We were assigned to sleep in two small rooms. I took the first one to the left across from the bathroom and noticed a window on the rear wall. In order to assume the leadership role in my group, I claimed the spot on the left closest to the door, laying my gear on the carpet.

We spent our time processing-in, performing guard and CQ duties, motor-pool truck maintenance, and physical training, at times wearing our gas masks during runs. Free time meant playing cards, volleyball, and football. Although I really enjoyed the latter, it left me sore, but I wouldn't accept preferential treatment.

Sniper fire was confirmed two days later on January 9, and the following morning we received word that we were on stand-by: Delta, the highest threat level, had been implemented.

On January 12, Sergeant Trost was listening to the Bills' 44-34 winning game over Miami, when President George H. W. Bush came on the air: "Congress has approved the use of force."

Trost thought D-Day was coming and wondered what was to come. That night, he prayed before bedtime: "God, help us all."

We were aware that a United Nations resolution had been passed on November 29, 1990, authorizing force against Iraq if it did not withdraw from Kuwait by January 15, 1991. Saddam Hussein had been given an ultimatum by President Bush— leave Kuwait or else. That day had come and gone without incident.

The night of January 16 brought Captain Huff and First Sergeant Fifer into our hallway. "Females, the first sergeant will give you something to drink. Drink it." We weren't told what it consisted of or why it was given.

We were each handed a small plastic cup of a green Kool-Aid-like liquid. "Begin taking your pyridostigmine bromide pills. You cannot get pregnant for a period of five years after taking these pills,"ordered the CO.

The PBs, as we called them, were used medically to treat

myasthenia gravis, a neuromuscular disorder that results in muscle weakness. The rectangular white package with black lettering did not, however, list myasthenia gravis as the reason for taking the pills; instead, it stated that the twenty-one tablets of pyridostigmine bromide, USP 30-mg pills, were nerve agent pre-treatment tablets. They could only be taken when a CO gave a direct order, which usually happened after receiving orders from higher-up that toxins had been discovered in the immediate area.

Since I was not planning on having children anytime soon, I wasn't worried, but a couple of the women wanted to have a child after re-deployment. One said, "Captain Huff, I want to have a baby when I get home. I don't want to take those pills."

He grimaced; his voice rose in volume as he glared at her. "That's a direct order, Specialist Laight."

Although the Food and Drug Administration had not approved PBs as treatment for nerve-agent poisoning, we took them as such. I did not question the order or the pills' efficacy; I recalled viewing slides of people affected by chemical exposure that showed gruesome blisters and burnt skin. If these pills could help reduce the devastating effects of chemical warfare, I was certainly taking them. The CO and the first sergeant remained with us until both were consumed.

On January 17, 1991, around 0300 hours Iraqi time (January 16, 1900 hours Eastern Standard Time), air strikes were launched against Iraq. Operation Desert Shield became Operation Desert Storm. Both presidents made comments: Bush declared the United States wouldn't fail, and Hussein threatened "the mother of all battles."

On the early morning departure to our base in the desert,

we had been awake about an hour when the first blaring NBC alarm sounded in wailing succession: *"Bweep! Bweep! Bweep!"*

"Shit!" said Sergeant Sara amid the noise, searching for her protective mask. I donned mine, following it with the visual signal—arms perpendicular to the body, hands cupped into fists, bringing them to my shoulders three times in rapid succession and yelling, "Gas, gas, gas!" This ensured that those who had not heard the alarm could see the cue and respond accordingly.

Within a few minutes, the threat level increased to MOPP level IV, the highest level of protection: protective over-garments, over-boots, and gloves. I quickly opened my MOPP suit packet and placed the protective clothing over my uniform, but when the open window in our room caught my attention, I signaled the nearest soldier to shut it. She shook her head and walked away; the person to her right did the same. No one wanted to close it and risk the possibility of being blinded by a nuclear blast; we could all have been harmed, though, so I secured it.

Chemical operations specialists overseas were continuously monitoring the environment for any traces of aerially deployed NBC weapons. When toxins were present, alarms sounded, leading soldiers to begin the masking process and enter the appropriate mission-oriented protective posture.

On December 5, 2000, the Pentagon's Special Assistant for Gulf War Illnesses, Medical Readiness, and Military Deployments sent notifications to members of selective units, including ours, that *Some Gulf War veterans may have been exposed to a very low level of chemical agent.* The most significant statement explained that some Iraqi rockets contained sarin and cyclosarin, chemical warfare agents. Stored in Khamisiyah,

Iraq, between March 10 and 13, 1991, the Special Commission for the United Nations later noted that Iraq's chemical stockpile included large quantities of cyclosarin. After receiving the all-clear order, we removed our masks and MOPP level clothing, continuing to our soon-to-be tented homes.

Our living conditions consisted of sandbags and concertina wire surrounding our base, and soldiers pulling eight-hour shifts of roving guard duty twenty-four hours a day on a daily basis. We pitched tents and laid wood-plank floors held down by pegs and sandbags. Our beds were sleeping bags on narrow foldable cots, over pneumatic, insulated cushions and small inflatable pillows. When it got cold, kerosene heaters provided limited warmth and we'd zip ourselves up, pulling coarse, itchy wool blankets over us.

Our unit's main but not sole job was to support the 82nd Airborne, 101st Airborne, 24th Infantry Division, 1st Calvary, 2nd Infantry Division, and the Marine Corps' 3rd Infantry Division. Usually when the 82nd and/or the 101st moved, we'd follow, pitch our tents, fill sandbags, and claim our usual spots.

Platoon sergeants relied on accountability; we were required to remain with our platoon for sleeping arrangements. Since each platoon contained between thirty and forty soldiers, a tent usually slept between ten and fifteen troops. In mine, I was the only woman.

Once settled in, we awaited the news for the first mission into Iraq, wondering who would initiate the assignment and hoping they'd come back alive. Returning with casualties from the onset would be an omen. Therefore, whoever went on the initial run had the unwanted pressure of avoiding a loss—something beyond any soldier's control.

# *16*

# Day By Day

THE PERSIAN GULF WAR CHANGED THE NOTION that fighting was solely for men or carried out on front lines. Female soldiers were now involved in hostile fire, held captive, and dying. The probability of women incurring an injury, held as prisoners of war, or killed in action had become a reality.

As acceptable as this may be for some, others do not agree. However, since war itself displays no prejudice, I do not think gender should be an issue, nor are women less capable. If one wishes to choose a combat specialty and successfully completes the same training as a man, she should be given the opportunity to do so. Just as restricting combat roles for females is outdated, moreover, so is requiring separate sleeping quarters in the battlefield.

A few days after settling into our tent, Burns, Lopez, Ross, and I were "cutting up," as Buddy would call it. Across from me, Burns sat next to Lopez, who was smoking a *beedi*, a small, thin Saudi Arabian cigarette.

Ross had just re-entered the tent, shuffling his feet on the way. When he sat down next to me, I roared, "You're not gonna do that shit again, right?"

"No, sista, I won't," he said, shaking his head.

"You better not! Keep your farts to yourself. Nobody wants to smell 'em. What the hell you eating anyway? We eat the same shit. You don't hear any of us suffocating people."

"Good Lord, Ross, what's wrong with you? You better get the medic to check you out." Chortling, Burns turned to Lopez. "I think Ross has a whole mess of whatchacall in his stomach."

Lopez took a drag, closed his eyes a bit, chuckling lightly.

"A whole lotta backed-up crap's what he's got. I never smelled anything like it. Let me tell you, Ross, you do that shit in the truck when we're riding together, and I'll throw you out."

"Come on, sista, I wouldn't do that." Ross grinned sheepishly. "I know you would throw me out, and it's a long way back to this hootch."

Guffaws started to diminish when Rides came down the wooden planks in a hurried manner. Bringing the pen he held in one hand up to his chin, he said without preface, "We're taking volunteers for the first mission into Iraq tomorrow."

The four of us looked up waiting for him to continue.

"You'll be assisting the 82nd Airborne." He raised the small notepad he held in his other hand to his waist. "Who wants to go?"

Patriot air strikes were frequent by then; Iraq had fired Scud missiles at Israel, but they had promised not to respond.

I rose from my cot. "I'll go."

Burns and Lopez stood.

"Me too, Sergeant," said Burns.

"And me," added Lopez.

Ross followed suit.

Rides nodded, "Okay." He turned, took a few strides, but stopped, as if forgetting something. He came back. Clicking the black Skilcraft government pen several times, he casually added, "Oh, make sure you have body bags."

"Yes, Sergeant," we replied, just before his abrupt departure.

We resumed joking, knowing that, if we were to die in a firefight, there was nobody else we'd rather be with.

News travels fast in a company, and soldiers learned about my volunteering. After chow that night, when Lopez, Ross, and I were squaring away our gear, Burns entered and approached me. "Torres, some of the guys asked me why you volunteered."

Standing with my double-stacked magazines' bandolier in my hand, I glanced at him. "And?"

"I said you wanted to."

I shrugged, making sure they were topped off. "Yeah? So?"

"You confused them," he chuckled.

"Why?" I asked, sitting on my cot to fill my army-green plastic canteens with the bottled water I had on hand.

"I don't know. I guess they didn't think a woman would volunteer."

"They don't know me."

"No, they sure don't," he laughed. Suddenly he expressed curiosity. "You know what Davis asked me?"

I looked up at him after removing my body armor and two grenades from beneath my cot. "What?"

"He asked me what you were running away from."

"What'd you tell him?" I stared, expressionless.

"I said, 'I don't know, Davis.' Strange question, huh?"

I shrugged and turned away, setting my gear on a nearby box that acted as my nightstand. I didn't answer Burns, who had no idea of the hovering demons; instead I asked, "Buddy, you got everything squared away?"

"I'm gonna do that now, Torres."

As I placed my Kevlar helmet over my utility belt, I thought of how perceptive that young private first class had been. In retrospect, I was running from something—the war in my mind that I wanted to keep at bay. I was unprepared for it, unwilling to confront it. The irony was that I was ready to face the consequences of the Gulf War, because I felt they were easier.

In the early morning hours that following day, the four of us set out to the Dhahran/Dammam Port to pick up the armored personnel carriers of the 82nd. Scud missiles often hit ports and airports, places we frequently transited. Our job was to meet with them at a predetermined point and join their convoy to one of the log bases in Iraq.

The four of us in similar garb—helmets over heads, gas masks at hips, chemical suits within reach—remained vigilant. While one drove, the other held a rifle, prepared to shoot.

The road we often traveled coined "Valley of Death" or

"Highway to Hell" was littered with fragmented, burnt, civilian and military vehicles. Charred weapons and scattered ammo lay strewn in the rear of pick-up trucks. Tanks and buses were spray painted *Fuck Saddam* and *Fuck Iraq*.

Enemy bunkers on the highway's overpasses, and random foxholes along the road, contained similar evidence of bombardment, their strategic positions further honing survival skills.

Now and then, bloated, decomposed bodies remained in vehicles where rigor mortis had set in. The stench that lingered in the air was very distinct, not only from those cadavers, but from the many others that had already been collected. It was difficult to describe yet recognizable.

Being in a war zone allows you to put things in perspective, making light of dangerous circumstances and appreciating the small comforts we take advantage of. Normal everyday bathroom events don't require etiquette, but craftiness is key, embarrassment non-existent, especially when it was time to have a bowel movement.

On one of the nights on that first mission into Iraq, Burns and I were standing by. Our truck's engine was off; we were stationed near a fire pit some rangers had made. Across the flame, the shadow of Lopez and Ross' truck faced in the opposite direction from ours.

While one of us slept lightly in a sleeping bag on the hood of the truck, or curled up on the front seat, weapon always at our sides, the other stood guard on the ground. Lack of sleep was a common factor, and we learned to sleep whenever we could, under whatever circumstance.

Tossing and turning inside our truck where I'd been attempting to take a nap, Mother Nature suddenly called. Adjusting my eyes to the darkness, I stuck my head out the window. "*Psst*, Buddy?"

Burns was coming around the trailer slowly, his weapon at port arms. "Hey." He stood by the passenger side door, looking up at my silhouette cast by the crescent moon. "You all right, Torres?"

"Yeah, but I gotta take a dump," I whispered, stepping out of the truck, weapon in hand.

"I'll get the sideboard."

We worked simultaneously. Leaning his weapon against the truck, he removed a sideboard from the trailer, propping it near the first set of duals. I slung my rifle across my back and removed an empty MRE box along with two full ones from the truck's underbelly. Together, we carved a hole through the empty one.

Standing the other two cardboard boxes on the hard sand, I placed the temporary toilet seat over them. Using the sideboard for concealment, I leaned my weapon on it and sat.

Stars twinkled in the clear desert sky amid the fire's soothing crackle and soft glow. Who would've thought, I wondered, that I'd ever find being in that kind of situation therapeutic? "Buddy?"

"What, Torres?"

"Can you hear me?" Then I caught myself. "Not taking a crap, I mean talking."

His low sneers were humorous. "Yes, Torres. I hear your voice."

"Imagine if the shit hits the fan now."

"Torres, what are you talking about?"

"I'd be caught with my pants down."

"Good Lord. You're a sick puppy."

I laughed.

Once completed, I tossed the box-filled feces with toilet paper into the fire pit.

"Alright, Buddy. It's my turn to stand watch. Go sleep, unless you gotta do your thing."

"No, Torres, I'm fine." He shook his head, adding, "I'll put the sideboard back on first."

Early the next morning, we resumed our convoy, driving in sandstorms with limited views of the vehicle in front of us. On foot, goggles helped us avoid the skin-nipping sand that flew in all directions from scratching our eyes. Regardless of the challenges we faced, there were always time for laughs: soldiers masquerading as raccoons once the goggles came off was amusing.

Bathing was another matter. Facilities were unavailable in Log Base Charlie in Iraq, and in Kuwait. Those were the lengthiest missions, but we learned to live with our body smell and kept hygienic by pouring drinking water into our Kevlar helmets to brush our teeth and wash our hair and privates.

While all this continued in Iraq, the war was well under way in Kuwait as U.S. troops captured the first Iraqi prisoners of war. Iraq continued firing Scuds at Saudi Arabia, and Patriots worked successfully at intercepting some; others remained a threat.

On January 23, 1991, Iraq torched the Kuwaiti oil wells, causing massive spills. Four days later, U.S. F-15s shot down Iraqi MIG-23s, and the *USS Louisville* became the first submarine to launch a cruise missile in combat.

We were on constant alert for NBC alarms, which usually

came before the Scuds, whose booming sounds indicated they had been deployed. Donning our masks multiple times a day and giving the visual signal was imperative, driving with them a challenge.

Once we arrived at our destination, we unloaded the APCs and returned to our base, relieved that our first mission had ended without casualties.

On another mission soon thereafter—this time with Specialist McMillian—the PB pills' side-effects began to emerge. We were continuously moving, stopping only to refuel or pee. Men were able to urinate anywhere. Even as their buddy drove, they'd open the passenger door. But the women had to stop. Frequently, McMillian had to pull over for me, and I started to notice a rash on the inside of my forearms, which I attributed to heat exposure.

On that mission, the depravity that shows lack of self-control became evident when McMillian and I were on standby. Having nothing to do, we began to verbally fight for fun. As he smoked his cigarette behind the steering wheel of our truck, I saw an older white soldier standing in my peripheral view outside our truck's right passenger door.

I knew what he was doing but chose to ignore it until the soldier spoke. "Te-rez, you look real perdy when you're mad— we gotta ride together. You turn me on. Keep talking."

It made me very uncomfortable, though I laughed, trying to play it off, but his actions were unmistakable. The soldier was jerking off near my window.

McMillian, clearly seeing my discomfort, asked, "What's he doing?"

Rolling my eyes and shaking my head, I answered, "You

don't wanna know."

"He's sick."

Saved by the bell minutes later, those in our convoy began moving their trucks, McMillian tossed his cigarette, and I was thankful to be rid of that scoundrel. The mission to drop off ammo to the 101st Airborne proceeded without incident.

Back at base, I was returning to my tent from the wooden stall showers when I saw Burns from afar.

"Hey, Buddy!" I waved.

We met each other halfway.

The awkward situation with the sergeant had remained on my mind. "Buddy?"

"Yes?"

"I don't know how to say this, but I gotta let somebody know, in case it gets worse."

"What Torres? Something happened with the PBs?"

"No, with Staff Sergeant Jarvis."

When I finished relaying the story, he shook his head. "Torres, you know you're dealing with sick, ignorant individuals here."

"Yes, but I'm outnumbered. Nothing's gonna be done in my defense, like at Eustis. I just wanted to let you know in case something happens to me. You can say what I told you."

"What'd McMillian say?"

"He was just as disgusted."

"Okay, Torres. You make sure you always tell me or Lopez."

"I will."

"Torres, let me ask you something. Do you feel safe?"

"Not a hundred percent, Buddy. We're supposed to be on

the same side. We just got here. It's gonna get worse."

Buddy grinned. "You're right."

"It'd be better if you rode with me. They're afraid of you, but not anybody else."

"I'll do everything I can, Torres, but you know it ain't up to me."

"I know that, Buddy. I know."

Suddenly changing the topic, Burns asked, "Torres, you still taking those pills?"

"The PBs?"

"Uh-huh."

"Yeah. Why?"

"A lot of troops are complaining about peeing too much and having whatchacall rashes on different parts of their bodies."

"Really?"

"Yes. Remember what Daddy said?" Based on his experience, Burns' dad, a Vietnam veteran, had warned him not to take any pills ordered overseas.

"Yeah, well, I already have those symptoms. I peed so much that McMillan asked me what was wrong. And look at this." I showed him the rash on my forearms.

"Good Lord. When'd you get that?"

"On this mission."

"Well, don't take anymore. The CO ordered the company to stop taking them. It came from Battalion."

"I already took a whole bunch, but I'll stop. Thanks for telling me."

Unfortunately, it was too late. Destructive damage had already begun to unfold inside my body.

# 17

# Opposing Forces

AVOC CONTINUED. On January 29, the Iraqi Fifth Mechanized Division attacked the Saudi town of Al Khafji,
eight miles south of the Kuwaiti border. The first Saudi force
that tried to counterattack was overrun, and despite our air
strikes, the Iraqis maintained control.

The following day the Saudis recaptured their town, causing the Iraqis to flee to the Kuwaiti border, while a marine battalion fired at Iraqi bunkers half a mile away in Kuwait.

The days and nights were moving along rapidly.

Aside from ordinary challenges, women had additional
ones. Managing our menstruation every month required common sense—storing used pads and having new ones on hand
was necessary.

Unlike men, women did not shave their heads—not that I
would've ruled it out if I had to. But as long as I could deal

with the sand fleas and other insects, I knew it'd be all right.

Being vigilant was a given. One cold night at camp, I was startled from sleep when I heard the distinct sound of propellers—not the norm. I intuitively gripped the rifle I slept with. Feeling for my gear—protective mask on my chest, grenades, extra ammo, and body armor beneath my cot—I wondered if anyone else heard it.

Leaning on my elbow, I turned my head to the cot on my right. Burns was snoring. "*Psst*, Buddy?"

"Huh, huh? Yeah?"

"Hear that?"

"Yup."

"How 'bout Lopez?"

Lopez was already up. "Yeah, I heard it."

"Ask Ross," I said.

"I'm awake. What's going on?"

"We don't know. Get your shit together. We might have to move fast," answered Lopez with ease.

Ross alerted the soldiers on either side of him.

Intensity in the dark air thickened at every turn of the blade. With quiet speed, we donned boots and gear, and stood by.

Around us, other soldiers were waking sound sleepers, making sure to not do so in an aggressive manner; the last thing anyone wanted was to be woken in haste and accidentally punch a fellow comrade.

The four of us waited on our cots, weapons at port arms—sandman in our eyes replaced by wide-eyed troops. I could sense we were all in the same state: eyes shifting from side to side, lips slightly parted, breathing in a controlled manner.

Then, silence. Just as the chopper had mysteriously appeared, it had left.

After ensuring it was gone for good, I asked, "What the hell was that?"

"I don't know. Strange, huh?" said Burns.

"Yeah," I answered as I heard Lopez nod—so acute had our senses become. No one slept at ease that night.

The next morning we learned it had been friendly aircraft. Our camp's position had not been compromised after all.

Base vigilance for me, however, didn't mean being watchful of the enemy only, but of some of my fellow troops as well.

One early evening, as I crossed out another day on my Richard Grieco calendar, Rides entered our tent, looking around. "Torres."

I looked over. "Yes?"

"You and Williams are going on a mission tomorrow. Go see Sergeant Perpis. Lopez, Ross, it's your turn for shit detail." He left.

I turned to Burns. "Hey, Buddy, how come you're not riding with me?"

He sat up, placed his feet on a wooden plank, and hesitated before responding. "I don't know, but the other day, First Sergeant said some soldiers have a problem with us riding together. He said they don't like it. They say I should give them a chance."

"A chance for what?" I asked indignant.

"I don't know. I said we get along, that we're both leaders," he replied.

"So what's the problem?"

"He says they're jealous."

"Jealous? Who? You keep saying 'they'. . .who are you talking about?"

"Some of the command, and some of the troops."

"But why do they care who I ride with?"

"Torres, they're sick, just like Jarvis." His eyes softened. "They don't understand how we can just be friends."

"You're kidding me," I scoffed. "Buddy, I didn't come here to get laid."

"I know that, Torres. You came here to do your job. That's what we're all supposed to do."

"So why can't we ride together all the time? Others do. Why us? Is it because you're black and I'm not?"

"That's part of it."

"And what else?"

"Well, they think of you sexually. Look, Sergeant First Class Woods said I've ridden with you enough, and I should let someone else get some. And Staff Sergeant Alley said it's okay if I'm getting some as long as I share. He says he knows women like you. They're the B-word." Buddy was not one to curse, no matter the situation.

"They would say that. . .those fuckin' dirt bags. And that Alley's scum," I smirked. "You know what he did in the showers the other day?"

"What?"

"He was using the stall next to me, and he moved closer to the wooden divider and asked if it would make me uncomfortable if he peeked over every once in awhile."

"What'd you tell him?"

"Nothing. I ignored him. Then someone came in to use the other shower and the bastard left."

"Did you have a problem with the other soldier?"

"No. . .Buddy, why can't they see me for who I am? I work harder and better than a lot of them."

"Torres, you're right. You're a better soldier than most, but they're afraid of us."

"They're not afraid of me when they do stupid shit like that."

"That's because they catch you alone."

I looked down and bit my thumb. "But why would they be scared?"

"Well, you're smart, you're not afraid, and you got that mouth. They're afraid of me because I'm big, and they don't want to see me go off on anyone. We're powerful together."

"But we're not doing anything wrong."

"No, we're not. We cut up all the time, try to keep people motivated, laughing. Torres, we are *leaders*. When you have two strong ones working together, others will follow, and that's what they don't want."

"Why not? That's good following."

Burns, ever patient, answered, "Yes, but then they'll see how bad this company is run, and they'll make complaints to Battalion. If they separate us, we can't set examples."

"Divide and conquer, huh?"

"Yes."

I sighed in frustration.

"You be careful on that mission, Torres."

"With Williams? Nah, he's all right." Williams was a quiet, thirty-something-year-old black man from Virginia. "It's poor Lopez and Ross who have to worry. They have shit detail." We ended that conversation with a laugh, but Buddy's words remained in the back of my mind.

Lopez and Ross would be conducting the daily shit detail. It consisted of two soldiers removing heavy metal drums from underneath the latrines. Once the contents were set on fire, the containers sat in open air. In the interim, the soldiers talked, smoked cigarettes, or both. About an hour later, they'd lift the receptacle by its handle, walk to the fire pit, dump it, and take turns stirring the feces with a street-sign-like pole until the possibility of airborne bacteria was removed.

I prepared for my mission with Sergeant Williams, not knowing where we'd go or if we'd be hauling food, water, mail, ammunition, POWs, APCs, or anything else. Afterward, I headed to the mess tent and grabbed a few MRE boxes for the trip, stowing them in our truck's underbelly.

Each package was contained in a brown plastic bag; its contents were warmed up on the hoods of our trucks or inside the interior vents. Favorites, such as potatoes au gratin (aka potatoes au rotten) and spaghetti and meatballs, made bartering common, but many agreed our greatest asset was the brownie dessert, not for its flavor but its utility: a pumice sponge for rough, cracked, calloused feet resulting from wearing combat boots in over-hundred-degree temperatures.

I went to speak with Perpis, a thirty-five-year-old white guy from North Carolina, who said it'd be a quick mission. We'd be dropping off ammo to the 1st Calvary at the nearest log base, returning independently once done.

The following morning, a few vehicles made up our convoy. The mission was conducted without incident; Perpis had been right—it was over fairly fast, and we returned to base on our own.

Williams and I went to buy incidental items at King Khalid Military City (KKMC), where there existed a makeshift American shop for soldiers.

We got back to base much later than expected. In the motor pool, we performed preventive maintenance and, before going our separate ways, turned in our logbook.

I strode along in the cool night air, blowing bubbles, swinging my plastic bag full of music cassettes, stationery, and munchies.

Private First Class Brown from Galax, Virginia, waved and headed towards me. "Hey Ter-rez," he called out in his low, refined drawl.

Standing in front of me, he said, "Burns and Lopez are looking for you."

"What for?"

"I don't know."

"Where are they?"

"By the mess hall."

From afar, lit by the interior lights, I saw them pacing outside the mess tent.

"Hey, guys! What's up? Brown said you were looking for me."

They stopped, turning at the sound of my voice. "Torres, where you been?" asked Burns. Deep lines marked his forehead, despite his look of relief.

"You're very late," added Lopez in soft reprimand, taking a few steps forward. His jaw clenched as he looked at me, expecting a logical explanation.

"Yeah. We finished early and stopped at KKMC to buy some stuff." I raised my bag. "See? What's going on? Why do you guys look so worried?"

"Haven't you heard?" asked Burns.

"Heard what? Just say it."

Lopez explained, "A male and female soldier from a transportation company got lost on a mission, and they were captured by the enemy."

I said nothing. *I wish it was me*, I thought. Why would I have desired such a thing? It's sad to recognize how insignificant my life was for me back then.

Burns sighed, "We thought it was you."

"Why?"

Lopez offered, "He was a sergeant, and she was a spec four."

"And you know Williams isn't the smartest soldier here," Burns interjected. He's always getting lost. We were coming up with a plan to go find you and bring you back."

"Really?"

"Yeah," they said, in unison.

I gazed at them. They were going to conduct a search-and-rescue for me, and there I was finding a way to self-destruct. I felt as if I had betrayed them.

Recognizing the dangers involved, they had decided our bond was strong enough for them to go through with it, and my brother Ross would've been right there, had he not been on a mission.

I'd have done the same for them. Had they left to look for me and lost their lives, I would've carried an enormous amount of guilt for the remainder of my life. Their behavior was incredibly humbling, true battle camaraderie, leading me to realize my death wish had to cease, not so much for me, but for them.

The irony was that, as much as their feelings were genuine, other troops still continued to sexually harass me. Ignoring my complaint stateside had indeed escalated overseas, bringing one or two of my buddies to escort me to the showers, use nearby stalls, or hover.

I added a machete that I had purchased in the desert to the knives and rifle that slept with me. For further protection, I strapped the rifle to my leg with a do-rag so that, if someone attempted to take it from me, I'd wake up and still be able to shoot.

It was obvious that troop paranoia had set in. Sooner or later something had to give, and I wondered how it'd all end.

# 18

# Depravity

"EVEN THOUGH I WALK through the valley of the shadow of death, I will fear no evil, for you are with me." The chaplain had begun service with Psalm 23. He looked up from the Bible he'd been holding, pausing at his audience. "That is where you are."

A tent served as our chapel; the hard benches of wooden picnic tables were our pews. Sleep deprivation was taking its toll, problems from home weighing on some, frustration between soldiers and the command was nearing its peak, myself included. There had to be a way out, and that was chapel service, which occurred sometimes on Sundays.

It was the only place soldiers sat in reverence, expressionless eyes looking up at the chaplain—the man who tried to keep hope alive—in his clean uniform and shaven face.

He resumed in his casual preaching style. "You have gone from the knowing into the unknowing, but God is omniscient. He knows what you need, and He will supply it when you need it most. Don't lose heart. Though you're in the valley of death, fear not. The Lord is with you, and you shall not lack. He will not forsake you." Although words were unspoken, it was clear everyone wanted God by their side, except the evil-doers; they were nowhere to be seen.

The chaplain was right. Even in dire moments, God had been with me, providing the way out of dangerous circumstances, blessing me with priceless friendships amid the cruelty. I appreciated the dog-tag cross charm, the inspirational cassette tapes, and desert camo Bible we'd been given, having paid much attention to Proverbs 24, which spoke of the hearts of evil men devising violence, their lips causing trouble.

I recalled verse 10: "If you faint in the day of adversity, your strength is small," and verse 16: "For the righteous falls seven times and rises again, but the wicked stumble in times of calamity."

I prayed that conditions wouldn't magnify, making me forget my beliefs in God and my unconditional trust in the three soldiers I loved most.

MY EXPERIENCES WITH FELLOW TROOPS in the Gulf resembled a ping-pong game. Every time I returned from a mission, something else would happen that would ignite the situation further.

Williams and I were headed back to base one day. Without any preface, he asked, "Ter-rez, can you do me a favor?"

Focused on the road, I glanced his way. "What?"

He looked away, appearing embarrassed. There was a pause before he said, "I'm getting tired of doing it all the time."

"Doing what?" I asked.

"Well, you know. . .it gets tiring after a while, to always, you know, do it to yourself."

In my peripheral vision, I saw him making a jerking-off motion. I couldn't believe what he was asking me to do. Williams kept to himself most of the time, and I hadn't expected that behavior from him.

Sarcastically, I replied, "That's why you have two hands."

"Two hands, huh?" he sneered. "Well, uh, Ter-rez, I was wondering if you could do it for me."

"Hell, no!"

Yet he persisted, "Why not?"

I was seething, but not wanting to cause an accident, I gave him a calm response. "I can't help you. That's a personal thing."

"If I'm asking you to do it, it's not personal. It's better when a woman does it."

That was it. "What! Go fuck yourself! You're lucky I'm driving."

He looked down.

I added, "Why you asking me? Gimme a fuckin' break. I get enough shit. Not you, too."

We drove to base in silence, but my head spun. I knew this couldn't be brought to the attention of the COC; nothing would be done. However, I did know someone who would do something—Burns.

Upon returning, I told him, and he went to speak with Williams immediately. The following day, Williams ap-

proached me as I was hanging up my laundry on the clothes-
line outside my tent.

"Hey, Ter-rez?"

"What now?" I answered, irate.

"I want to apologize for the thing yesterday. I was way
off. I'm sorry. I don't know what I was thinking. It won't
happen again."

"That's *right* it won't." I stopped adding clothes to the line,
and said, "I didn't expect that from you, Williams. You were
all right in my book."

"I'm sorry, Ter-rez. I apologize."

"Okay. Just forget it."

"Thank you, Ter-rez."

"You're welcome."

We had no further problems; however, curious to know
what had compelled him to apologize, I entered my hootch to
speak to Burns, who'd been listening to music.

"Williams just apologized. What'd you tell him?" I asked,
placing the pail under my cot.

"I told him he wasn't a man. Real men are able to control
themselves."

"That's it?" I sat.

"Well, I said he was selfish, only thinking of himself, and
asked him if he'd like someone to ask his wife, sister, or daughter to do that."

I shook my head. "So you just attacked his character?"

"Yes. Why? What'd you think I said?"

"I thought you threatened him."

"No, uh-uh. A man tells another man that he's not a man,
and that is sometimes enough."

For Buddy, it had been that simple. He was a family man who had integrity, but, unfortunately, many did not.

In addition to me, though not to my extent, other women were also harassed. They were just as frustrated as I was with the lack of attention the matter was receiving.

The problem with men and women together in combat, whether officers or enlisted, is that some men want to exert power over women while others find it difficult to accept them as soldiers and think of them as sexual objects instead. Naturally this does not apply to the majority of troops I have known or know of, but it only takes a few bad apples to spoil the batch.

Complaints are made against the rotten ones, yet they are seldom resolved appropriately; they are, instead, ignored. Sometimes the victim is deemed a troublemaker or crazy, given a counseling statement, or sent to mental health for screening.

The issue is then swept away; the woman is transferred, or medically discharged, making her feel like the culprit. She has a less than fruitful or ruined career, and the guilty party's actions are not addressed. The cycle then continues.

Victims are left distraught and hopeless, no longer believing in the organization they once trusted and forced to pick up the broken pieces of their lives alone.

But sex crimes in the military are not limited to women. Despite their size or strength, men are also victimized. Their silence is further heightened by the fact that they are men and considered to be the "stronger" sex. If one is brave enough to report it, he risks chastisement and disregard from his chain of command. It's as if the complainant gets penalized for speaking the truth.

When the "Don't Ask, Don't Tell" policy was lifted, my stomach churned as I thought of the men and women who'd enlist, choosing to express their sexual preferences without considering the consequences. I thought of the isolation and ridicule that could follow, as well as the harassment and rapes that could be committed. Although I understand a person's desire to speak up, being vocal has a price.

I believe the most effective manner to handle military sexual trauma is by appointing civilians to handle them, thus removing coercion by higher ranks. Moreover, it is vital that enlistees are informed of this potential problem beforehand and provided precise information on who can help.

Change will begin the day a strong civilian structure exists that punishes perpetrators appropriately. Until then, these issues will resurface.

TWO EARLY MORNINGS LATER, on a mission in a small convoy while Lopez drove with blackout lights, I was sitting at port arms when we came to a standstill. There was repeated hostile fire ahead.

We turned slowly to face each other, saying nothing. Our trucks were loaded with ammunition, food, and water, for the 2nd Infantry Division. We knew a decision had to be made between completing the mission and safeguarding the troops.

First Lieutenant White, the officer in charge, neared each vehicle, whispering, "Stand by. We're waiting for orders from higher up."

If we moved forward, the rumbling engines would reveal our position. My thoughts were racing. *Let's do it—we're gonna die if we do—so this is how I'm gonna die.*

I was indifferent, but thought it a shame that my life would be taken by violence twice. It appeared I'd never have a chance at happiness. Yet in that moment, I welcomed death: The peace I'd once had would finally be restored.

White came down the row of trucks again as I was entertaining these dismal thoughts. "Fall back," he said.

My sentiments were in conflict—disappointment that I wouldn't get to fight, and a slight relief that I hadn't. Perhaps I had begun to value my life.

As if being sexually harassed didn't teach me enough about humanity's degradation, I learned another important lesson in life: War tests a man's true character.

One late afternoon in the mess tent, as I put my empty plate and cup with the dirty dishes, Burns walked up to me, hands in his pockets. "Torres, I gotta tell you something."

"What?"

"Not here." He looked around with concern.

"Okay. Where?"

"Just walk with me."

I followed him outside, down rows of tents, where boxers, t-shirts, and BDUs were drying on clotheslines. He led me toward the motor pool and stopped near the farthest trailer.

"Okay, Buddy. What's the mystery?"

"Hold on." He looked around. Distinct sounds of clanging and murmurs by maintenance personnel had become whispers in the wind.

"What's going on?"

"Torres, you gotta watch yourself."

Exasperated, I asked, "From what? What are you talking

about?"

"Some guys wanna harm you."

"*Who? Why?*"

Buddy looked anxious.

"Come on, Buddy, just say it."

He let out a sigh. "Look, I was walking around, staying to myself, you know how I do, and I heard some guys talking."

"And?" I twirled my hand to rush him along. Buddy was big, but he sure was slow.

"And they mentioned your name."

"Who did?"

"You know, Pitts, Earl, Snell, Tapirs, whatchacall. . . ." He snapped his fingers, trying to remember. "You know, the one with the beady eyes and messed-up teeth."

"Brady?"

"Yeah, that one."

"And? What'd they say?"

"They were talking about them all being on a mission with you. If they got into a firefight, they'd rape you."

"*Rape* me?"

"Yes."

"What'd they say *exactly*?"

"They said, 'Yeah, let's rape Ter-rez. If we're all on a mission, and getting shot at, we can rape her.'"

"Who said it first?"

Burns shook his head in defeat, letting out a breath. "I don't know. I didn't hear that part. They were already talking when I heard them."

"They all agreed?"

"Yes, Torres. They all said they'd do it."

Having gone through the devastating effects of my 1985 rape, I wasn't going to let that happen again. I paused before remarking, "Buddy, don't worry. I can at least kill two or three of them before they knock me out. You know I got a lot of rounds. I ain't going down without a fight."

"I just wanted you to know, Torres. So you can be on alert."

"Thanks, Buddy. I'll be all right. They got another thing coming." Suddenly, I thought of something. "Buddy, if I die after taking some of them down, make sure you have an investigation opened and take it to the top. The command here will make up some bullshit to make me the culprit just to cover their ass."

Though Burns' information was crucial, giving it lots of thought could've brought tunnel vision, which might have made me less aware of my surroundings. I knew this had to be addressed in the civilian sector.

The next time I called home, I briefed Mom and told her to contact my unit for assistance in opening an investigation through the senator in New Jersey. I asked her to have Marlene, who was living in Florida, follow the same protocol.

Unfortunately, and without telling me, Mom didn't immediately follow through with my request. She erroneously believed I'd be further jeopardized, and told my sister to do the same.

In the interim, as I waited for some type of reprieve, I become more watchful of those five soldiers. My vigilance took on a different light. A crime was now a crude possibility, leading me to ponder the most critical question: Whom can I trust?

# *19*

# Casualties

**M**Y BELIEFS ARE STRONG: An honorable soldier should be upheld and treated with utmost respect. Whether one agrees with the reasons for war is not as important as providing troops with support. Our freedom has never come, nor will it ever, without cost; visible and invisible consequences always follow. The Persian Gulf War was no different.

On February 22, 1991, President George H. W. Bush demanded Iraqi troops withdraw from Kuwait by noon the next day, or else. President Saddam Hussein's troops stayed. Perhaps he believed the ultimatum had been a bluff when nothing happened.

However, an allied ground offensive began at 0400 hours on February 24 Saudi time after President Bush authorized General Norman Schwarzkopf to employ all available forces to expel the Iraqi army from Kuwait.

The first day's strategies were a dramatic success, though Hussein, knowing the capability of his enemy, ordered his troops to resist with all their might. As a result, on Saturday, February 25, an Iraqi Scud missile plummeted into American barracks in Dhahran, Saudi Arabia. The total deceased, injured, or traumatized, is not something I'd dishonor by noting the casualties. Let's just say that lives were destroyed.

The 26th of February brought forth the third largest tank battle in history—the Battle of 73 Easting. The U.S. 2nd Armored Calvary Regiment was involved in the central part of the battle, leading the way and performing recon for the Army's VII Corps. Other American and British units were also involved in this endeavor.

Despite aircraft grounded by howling winds that created a sandstorm forming limited visibility, the Iraqis' 18th Mechanized Brigade, and the 37th Armored Brigade, were attacked and destroyed, causing Iraq's loss of over 160 tanks.

Meanwhile, Iraq's militia set hundreds of oil wells on fire in Kuwait. From a driver's vantage point at a distance, burning oil flames shot into the air covering the sunlit sky with large, thick black clouds of smoke. If one hadn't known any better, you would have sworn it was nightfall. Many of us did not realize what the exposure to those fumes could have brought, until it'd be too late.

One of the biggest missions in United States military history consisted of a convoy that extended for many, many miles. Different U.S. branches, and allied forces, worked jointly to enter Iraq with tons of reinforcement. Trucks full of weapons, ammo, medical supplies, APCs, food, and water were on standby.

We were staged in Salman Pak, outside Baghdad, when an officer ordered, "If you engage the enemy, shoot to kill."

Sitting on the passenger side of our truck, wearing my bullet-resistant vest, rifle in hand, gas masked strapped on my right thigh, I turned to Burns. "This is it." I was stoic.

Yup." He nodded.

Trucks idled; soldiers maintained high-intensity anticipation as we waited for our superiors to speak the two words that would change our future: *Move out.*

Insurmountable repercussions were a strong possibility. The sound of engines would alert the enemy. Vehicles would be disabled when struck by fire. Casualties would be high, and those who survived would continue to fight until either side was killed or captured.

The wait seemed interminable. Burns and I had just stepped out of our vehicle to stretch our arms and legs. On the desert sand in the blazing heat, I looked at him through the open door, thinking how we mimicked each other. Neither one of us could have hoped for a better battle buddy.

He glanced my way; the words he'd written on the band around the cover of his Kevlar helmet stared at me: *You do me wrong, I do better.* They would later prove to be an omen for us.

When our eyes locked, we read each other's minds: *What's taking so long?*

We were still standing near the trailer's front tires when indecipherable shouting made us turn. Burns appeared at my side. Around us, soldiers were incredulous.

"What'd he say?"

"Huh?"

"What the fuck?"

We were still trying to make out the words when the preposterous shouts became clear. *"The war's over!"* Williams yelled from afar, arms flailing, smile beaming.

The disbelief on my face caught his attention. "Hey, Terrez, the war's over."

"Get the fuck outta here! Where'd you hear that?"

I looked at Burns, whose eyebrows were raised. "Command just sent word to soldiers in the field. There's a cease fire." Williams did not tarry. He wanted to share the good news with other troops.

That was fast, I thought.

Rifle loosely in hand, Burns opened the passenger door.

"What are you doing?" I asked, offended.

He raised his weapon. "Well, we won't be needing this anymore."

Still gripping mine, I stared at him.

"What's wrong?" he chuckled, stopping beside me, unarmed.

"You mad?"

"No. I'm disappointed."

"You were ready, huh?"

"Of course." My mind and body were in sync with my adrenalin. Now I had to decompress; I felt confused, frustrated. I should've been happy, but I wasn't. *How could I be in a war and not fire my weapon?* I felt like a fraud.

"Well, be glad you're all right."

I sighed. The movement of troops in retreat brought me to reality. "Buddy, I'll drive." As quickly as the news came, we mounted our vehicles to return to base, our mission aborted.

The desert's panoramic view seemed a paradox; the hundreds of thousands of miles previously driven under hostile fire and wailing alarms would now be conducted for redeployment amid herds of camels, either held by a bedouin's embroidered strap or moseying alone on the road.

Shepherds, dressed in free-flowing *thobes* with *ghoutras* on their heads and *na'als* on their feet, led their sheep. Natives knelt on small rectangular rugs facing eastward to offer their *salah* after hearing the screeching echoes signaling their prayer time.

Bedouin tents of various sizes were backdrops for smiling children who waved to soldiers driving rigs. When able, we'd make hand peace symbols, slow down, and toss them candy. Nearby women in *burqas* expressed gratitude with their eyes. Civilians were no threat to us, as they would be in the later war.

Realizing our mission was really over, I began to shift my frame of mind. Home was now something reachable, but I did not know if I cared to return. Being in country had changed all of us. My friends and family were the same, but I was not. How do you transition from a constant state of vigilance to a normal, unruffled life?

At base, we had learned that Iraqi forces had retreated on February 26. President Hussein had announced the complete withdrawal of Iraqi occupation. The following day, President Bush had declared suspension of offensive combat, laying out conditions for a cease-fire, thus liberating Kuwait.

The Gulf War had been successful, yet a price had been paid: There had been wounded soldiers, battle-related deaths, non-combat deaths, troops missing in action, as well as held prisoners of war.

In addition, nearly half of the deployed service members, me included, would later become afflicted with Gulf War Syndrome.

Though war had ended, my battle with ignorant leadership was yet to end. It angered me that I had to remain defensive, cautious of some fellow troops, while those same soldiers continued to behave without a care. I took correspondence courses on civil disturbance, weapons, and infantry in the meantime, but I wondered when life would be normal for me again.

Rumors about redeployment dates ran amok, each more far-fetched than the last, leading to frustration. One way to let off steam was to get together and fight each other for sport.

Burns and the second biggest guy in the company, a sergeant from North Carolina, Kitts, often tag-teamed others to knock them down. Burns, the bigger of the two, hadn't been taken down yet and, at times, a group of soldiers would jump him from behind in an attempt to do so.

One afternoon, after completing my daily duties, a crowd huddled near the maintenance area. Curious, I strolled over to the six soldiers who'd formed a circle. In the center, Burns and Kitts were fighting five of the guys, and the dynamic duo wasn't losing. "Hey!" I shouted with authority. "Stop!"

Everyone paused, looking over in my direction.

"Burns, you can't be messing with maintenance."

"Well, Torres, they jumped us," he said, straightening up. Others followed.

"That's right," added Kitts, the truth in his small blue eyes evident.

"That's cause they're sick of you guys jumping everybody and not being able to knock you down." I pointed at Buddy.

Kitts glanced over at Burns, who was laughing. "It's not my fault they can't take me down. Maybe they need to change their diet."

Feet firm on the ground, shoulder-width apart, I challenged him: "I can take you."

Amid whispers and murmurs, Burns asked with incredulity, "*You?*"

He glanced at Kitts, who raised his brows and shrugged. "Who else? Come on. Let's fight. Me and you."

"Is that what you wanna do, fight?"

"That's what I said. I don't stutter."

Plenty of laughter and "oohs" followed.

"All right then," said Burns.

The five soldiers who had been inside the circle joined the six spectators.

Action is faster than reaction. I didn't wait. I'd been watching Burns' tactical style since Eustis. Knowing his weakness, I was going to use it to my benefit.

Burns was right dominant, so I went for his left wrist with my right hand, aiming at his pressure point. He turned his hand over; now it was on mine.

Instinctively, I elbowed his stomach hard with my left arm, using my shoulder for more power, surprising him. Then I second-guessed his next move—right foot forward, trip my ankle, and drop me to the ground, where I'd fall like a rag doll.

Pivoting on my right foot, leaning my body, I kicked his shin with my left foot, thankful to be wearing combat boots. He shuffled back two paces, losing his grip on my forearm, and came at me with force. I rapidly ducked low to my right. He missed me by a fraction, losing his equilibrium, and I seized the opportunity to move in fast by slamming my body onto his with all the strength I could muster.

In the blink of an eye, Burns had fallen on his back with a loud thump. With perspiration rings underneath his arms, swirling sand coming up from him like dust on a chalkboard, I clapped my hands. "Ha!"

I scanned at the crowd of soldiers in different states of surprise—shaking heads, jaws dropped, hand over mouths. It was hilarious!

Brown had been one of the observers. His curious dark brown eyes widened; his voice rose a few octaves when he brought his hands together. Clapping, he shouted, "Oh my word! She did it!"

Off he went. "Hey, everybody! Hey, everybody!" He continued to clap, yelling repeatedly between the lines of tents at anyone and everyone. "Te-rez knocked Burns down!"

That was all Burns needed to hear to be further humiliated. He remained still on the ground, and I couldn't help but laugh at his dumbfounded expression.

I teased, "See? I told you, you were slow."

That had been Burns' downfall; although he was big and strong, he wasn't quick and agile. It was an epic moment; I wanted to revel in it.

Face, mouth, and bald head full of sand, hat having fallen off to the side, he looked at me, shock and embarrassment clear. "I'm gonna kill you, Torres."

I laughed loudly, extending my hand, grinning. "Need help?" When he shook his head, I shrugged and walked away.

Time moved fast; it was difficult to keep track of what day it was. It's not surprising that some of us have recollections others don't. For Burns, it was passing an overturned tarpless truck on the way to a friendly Kuwaiti mission.

The soldier had tried to avoid a collision; as a result, the truck had flipped. He was lying on the ground to the right of his vehicle. Once Burns noticed him, he and a few other soldiers screeched to a stop.

He leapt out to perform CPR, but the soldier was bleeding from his left ear, and he understood a traumatic brain injury had been sustained. Fearing his condition would worsen, Burns decided not to provide it.

At that point, the troop made eye contact with him. In slow, clear speech, he said, "Tell my family I love them."

"You're gonna be all right," Burns encouraged him. "Help's coming."

Another soldier had waved to a British MedEvac helicopter. Once it landed, Burns carried the injured soldier onto it amid swirling sand, propellers spreading the hot desert air. He walked away and looked back, but when he saw the soldier's arm slump, Burns knew he was gone.

Every troop who sees another die retains the memory. Burns was no different.

There had been no name tag on his uniform; rather, his jacket, containing a 1st Cavalry patch, was inside the truck. However, Burns has never been able to relay that message. He still hopes to locate the family one day. Until then, he will continue to carry that weight with him.

# 20

# No Relief

**M**USIC POURED OVER THE BOOM BOX belonging to Specialist McGirt, a black male volunteer from Brooklyn. In our platoon's hootch, four sets of grubby hands were playing Spades on a makeshift cardboard table after a sandstorm.

Wearing t-shirts, cargo pants, and flip-flops, some of us sat on cots smoking pungent beedies, while others sang, tapped feet, or snapped fingers in synchronicity.

"Come on, Buddy...pay attention! They're beating us!" I yelled.

"Well, Torres, I *am* paying attention. I just can't get a good hand," said Burns, shaking his cards in frustration.

"Buddy, use your head. Maybe you should take off that do-rag. It might be compressing your brain."

"That's right." McGirt laughed, before taking a puff.

"Set 'em up," I said to Burns.

"Well, I would if I had something to set them up with."

I was pissed. We had been on a roll; two other teams had already been defeated. I didn't want to lose. "Buddy, gimme a break," I said, exasperated. "Stop making excuses. If we lose, it's gonna be your fault." I pointed a finger at him.

McGirt egged me on. "You tell him, Torres."

Lopez chuckled.

"McGirt, shut up. This is between me and Torres." Burns was clearly frazzled.

"McGirt," I interjected, "can say whatever he wants. He's exercising his first amendment rights."

"Thanks Torres," smiled McGirt.

"You're welcome. . .and don't go picking on McGirt just 'cause he's smaller than you." McGirt stood about 5'7" and weighed no more than 140 pounds.

Burns rolled his eyes and shrugged his shoulders. "Good Lord, I ain't picking on anybody, Torres."

Lopez was quiet. He took my rants in stride.

McGirt, on the other hand, laughed and cheered me on when I gave Burns a hard time.

Like a displaced lighthouse cutting through fog, Rides suddenly entered our tent. "Too much smoke in here," he said, waving his hands through the air while moving his head to and fro. "Torres, the CO would like to see you in the lead tent."

Our rowdy game became silent. As I looked up at him, cards in hand, I saw Burns squint, Lopez raise an eyebrow, and McGirt drop his mouth.

"For what?" I asked.

"A verbal counseling session," Rides replied impassively.

"For *what?*"

He shrugged. "You have to be there in twenty minutes."

"But why? You should know, Sergeant."

"I don't know, Specialist Torres. I have to be there, too."
He turned and walked away.

Burns spoke first. "He's up to no good, that devil."

"Yup," Lopez agreed. "You better watch yourself."

"Man, what are you gonna do?" McGirt asked with concern.

"I'm gonna go." I frowned and looked across at Burns.
"Buddy, I'm gonna borrow your Walkman."

"Okay."

"Walkman for what?" questioned McGirt.

"Don't worry about it. Let's keep playing. Come on,
Buddy. And you guys better not feel sorry for me by letting
me win. I'll get pissed."

"I wouldn't do that to you," said Lopez.

"Me neither. I don't want you mad at me," McGirt added.

Although my buddies were true to their word, the game
wasn't the same; we all wondered what had prompted the CO
to order a counseling session.

Burns and I lost, but I didn't give him any grief.

The tension in the tent was thick as McGirt shuffled to
his cot, boom box off, Lopez moved the boxes to the side, and
Burns made sure his Walkman cassette player was in proper
working order. He and Lopez instinctively knew what I had
in mind.

"Okay, Torres. It works."

"Is it a new tape?"

"No, but it's blank."

"Did you put tape on both ends?"

"Yes I did. I tested it, too."

"Not for nothing, Buddy, but I wanna make sure."

"All right, I know these ignorant men have got you all paranoid."

Burns was referring to the night our convoy had rested inside the trucks on a mission. I'd napped while he remained awake behind the steering wheel. I had punched him hard in the middle of my sleep, but I hadn't been aware of it until he'd told me the next day. He'd remained still until I had fallen asleep again.

He pressed *play*. Burns' slow strong voice sang a beautiful symphony: "Testing, one, two. Testing."

"Torres. . ." he began, handing me the square black-and-silver recording device that would be my ammunition. His eyes widened, and his tone dropped a notch. "You be careful. I don't like this."

Lopez, who was standing next to me, agreed. "I don't like it either. Don't get caught."

"Guys, don't worry. I'll be fine. I'm not doing anything wrong—this isn't illegal. I'm protecting myself, and I'll be walking in holding this in plain view."

"Just be careful, Torres," warned Burns. "There's no telling what he's up to."

"We'll be watching. Anything happens, you let us know somehow." The muscle in Lopez' jawline tightened, confirming the seriousness of what I was about to do.

"I will. I'm turning this on the minute I leave here. Gotta get ready."

Moments later, I walked out holding the Walkman and

pressed the record button. The small red light went on. Every step I took on the packed sand underscored the importance of staying focused. I was going to get every single word on tape. I'd show them not to mess with me.

From afar, my enemies stood outside the tent's entrance: Captain Huff and his henchman, Rides, and two senior NCOs from third platoon, Staff Sergeant Mudd and Staff Sergeant Wilbur. I began to speak their names into the recorder, moving my head to make-believe music in case someone was watching me.

I stood before them.

"Specialist Ter-rez, follow us so we may begin," the CO said curtly as he entered.

I walked behind Rides, remaining calm. Mudd and Wilbur followed.

Folding chairs had been pre-set. The CO got right to the point. "Specialist Ter-rez, your relationship with Sergeant Burns is decreasing the morale of the troops." He paused.

The recorder in my hands figuratively morphed into a high-power rifle.

"I will not run this company with impropriety," he resumed.

I maintained my composure while asking in a flat, clear voice, "What kind of relationship are you talking about, sir?"

He flinched. Had it been a laughing matter, I would've found his reaction comical.

He enunciated each word. "I don't need to give you an explanation, Specialist Ter-rez. When the company commander perceives there is a problem, there is a problem." He glared at me, hatred clear in his beady blue eyes. "If the company commander says there's a relationship, there's a relationship."

A few seconds lapsed as we stared each other down. Rides looked away; Mudd moved his eyes around; Wilbur took a sudden interest in a piece of paper he'd been holding.

The CO vehemently added, "I don't need to explain myself to you. You will be moved from second platoon to third platoon. Staff Sergeant Mudd is present for Sergeant First Class Wratt, your new platoon leader, who is currently on a mission. Staff Sergeant Wilbur will be your new squad leader."

I turned my head toward Mudd and Wilbur, thinking of what poor excuses for leadership they were, knowing a gross exaggeration of power was taking place, yet none uttered a word in my defense, Rides included. Not one of them met my eyes.

"After this meeting, Staff Sergeant Wilbur will follow you to your tent, where you will have twenty minutes to remove all your belongings to the female tent. You are prohibited from speaking to Sergeant Burns," concluded the CO.

The rules had been changed again while I was away on the last mission. Separate showers had been installed, and all eleven women had been ordered to move into one tent.

I said nothing. The counseling session had been oral, proving it was wrong and baseless, but questions rumbled through my mind. *Why me and Burns? How come he wasn't called in?*

If there was any such decrease in morale, it was due to the man's inconsistencies and debasing commentaries as a leader. I wasn't going to accept his maltreatment. "Sir, at this time, I'd like you to know I'm taking this further up my chain of command."

"Specialist Ter-rez, you may very well do so when you have time off from your missions." He rose, declaring the meeting over.

As I exited the tent, I heard Wilbur's voice from behind. "Specialist Ter-rez, will you come here?"

*Now what?*

I turned and saw him signaling to the right side of the tent. "Welcome to third platoon," he said in hurried edginess. "I'd like you to sign this statement." Hands shaking, he held out the pen and document he'd been inspecting.

"What is it?"

"It addresses your duties."

"What duties?"

"Your duties as a member of third platoon."

"I'm a truck driver. The duties are the same in all four truck platoons."

Ignoring my remark, he said, "Specialist Ter-rez, I'd like you to be in proper uniform at all times."

"I'm always in proper uniform, Sergeant Wilbur."

"The statement says that you agree to remain in uniform at all times."

"Even during down time?"

"Yes," he answered lamely.

"That's not right. Why am I being singled out?"

Standard male boxers were issued to both sexes, which were neither short nor tight. During free time, we could wear them or civilian clothes.

"Because it will be easier, Specialist Ter-rez."

"Easier for who?"

"For you."

"For me?" I asked, indignant.

"Yes. Specialist Ter-rez, please do me the favor and just sign."

I exhaled, knowing I couldn't refuse; not complying with a senior NCO's request would bring me additional problems. All I could do was wait to take it to Battalion, which would prove to be another feat.

Later that day, I relayed the news to Lopez, who would be the messenger between Burns and me until we called the CO's bluff in a week. In the meantime, they went to Battalion to file complaints.

In order to prevent me from going further up the COC, I sensed, I was continuously being sent out on missions. My suspicions were confirmed when another soldier overheard the CO say, "Keep the bitch on the road."

Luckily, in third platoon, I was partnered with Sergeant Trost, a white guy from New York who had volunteered. We had similar mindsets, and I enjoyed our conversations. I admired the manner in which he respected everyone. Often, on missions, we spoke of life and his wish to return to college. It was comforting to hear his low, soft voice; I took our partnership as my respite after being exposed to such wanton hostility.

I was resilient, though. After returning to base early from a mission about two weeks later, I wasted no time. I quickly went to speak to a chaplain at Battalion, who directed me to Inspector General Major Essex. I brought the tape.

Major Essex listened; mentioning the tape stirred him. I could see by his reaction—deer in headlights—that he tried to envision the chaos it could cause.

Once I finished, he said, "Specialist Torres, I will need you to give me that tape in order for me to hear it and speak with my superiors accurately."

It seemed a ruse, but he'd been the next step in my chain of command; I had nowhere else to go. I removed it from my pocket. "Sir, when may I have it back?"

"You may come by tomorrow at ten hundred hours."

"Sir, what if I get sent out on a mission? It can be days before I can come and get it."

"Specialist Torres, I will speak with your commanding officer and ensure you do not get sent out on any missions until you have the tape in your possession. What would you like done?" he asked.

"I'd like a written counseling statement to go in the chain of command's files, sir."

"We're not looking to punish anyone, Specialist Torres."

Pathetic, I thought. *What about me?* I was mad, but I didn't show it. I handed the tape to him, expecting the worst but hoping for the best.

# 21

# Uphill Battles

McGIRT AND MANNING FILED their own complaints at
Battalion. More soldiers followed; Burns had been right.

One night soon after, I entered the orderly tent to mail a
letter to Lieutenant Colonel Oliver North regarding my sexual
harassment complaint. Seated around various denominations
of bills piled in the center of a table were the CO, White, the
First Sergeant, a sergeant, and two specialists playing cards.

What unashamed hypocrisy, I thought, as I left to talk to
Lopez, who was smoking a cigarette outside the mess tent.
"Hey."

He read my face. "What's up, Torres?"

"The CO and White are gambling with NCOs in the orderly tent."

"Okay, I'll get Burns. We'll take pictures."

"Make sure you get the money on the table. Watch your

back."

"We will. Wait for us in your tent. We'll call you out."

About twenty minutes later, sitting on my cot with ears perked up, I heard Lopez' voice. "Torres?"

I left and strode between them across the dark desert. "Well?"

Lopez's eyes were gleaming. "We got them all, Torres."

Burns added, "Money on the table, too."

"Great. How soon can the film get developed?"

"I'm going on a mission tomorrow. I'll find a way to get it done," said Burns.

"Thanks, guys. It'll be good to have in case any of us needs it."

"That's right," agreed Lopez.

My buddies and I knew the time had come to disclose the gambling that we had witnessed, as it violated Army Regulation 600-20, namely, no gambling between officers and enlisted personnel.

We called it a night and returned to our tents.

When I headed to Battalion a few days later, I stopped at the sinks near the latrines to brush my teeth and saw Manning. "Hey, Manning."

"Hi, Torres, I'm going to Battalion to follow up on my complaint. Are you going now?" she asked.

"Yes. Wanna go together?"

"That'd be great."


OUR TRIP TO BATTALION had two purposes: I had to get my tape, and she was going to request to speak with a Judge Advocate General (JAG) Officer. Nothing had been resolved regarding her complaints either.

At what point does anyone in command do something? There were no women of high rank to turn to, and the men did nothing but listen with closed ears.

In my cargo pocket was the gambling evidence I would bring to air force MPs after the tape was in my possession.

We approached the major, who was standing outside a tent. "What are you here for?" he asked me with contempt.

"I'm here to pick up the tape, sir."

"Oh, that tape. Didn't I give it to you?" he mocked.

"No." *Jerk.*

Without saying another word, he turned to Manning. "Go in and have a seat," he said curtly.

After a short while, the major came out holding my tape loosely in his left hand. "This tape?" he asked, before handing it to me.

"Yes, sir." I hoped it hadn't been tampered with.

I headed to the nearest MPs and provided a statement and the clearest photograph. Once that was done, I returned to base.

That week, when Trost and I finished our next mission early, I went to see a colonel at Army Central Command. The salt-and-pepper haired officer's commanding presence gave me mixed emotions as I sat across his desk describing my plight from the inception. *Will he help?* I searched his face for a reaction: bored and impatient.

It was difficult to explain sexual harassment to a man. Most didn't understand it completely or didn't care to. My perception was that he presumed I was another disgruntled female soldier trying to stir things up in a predominantly male world.

In the end, there were more barricades. Having had a slew of experience, the colonel, who could've done something, took no action.

The roller coaster continued when I learned about the outcome of the gambling investigation. The officers received a reprimand, and nothing was written in their files. Afterward, the first sergeant put the word out that there would be no more gambling, and that was that. I felt defeated. It is no wonder that soldiers remain silent over so many injustices; nothing seems to get done right.

Just when I thought there'd be no respite, I received a letter from a captain in my home unit. It contained my promotion to sergeant, signed by a lieutenant colonel; a copy had been sent to command overseas.

Knowing I had met the requirements for sergeant and aware of the disservice I was experiencing, they had decided to send my promotion orders. I was ecstatic and got some rank from Manning to place on my lapel, but it was short-lived.

Before leaving on my next mission, the CO approached me with Lt. Pugh. "Specialist Ter-rez, remove your rank."

"Why, sir?"

"The orders have to go to me directly."

"They were sent to Battalion, sir."

Pugh interjected, "It's not clear if they were sent to the 32nd commander."

"Until it is made certain through telephone calls, you cannot wear your rank. Do you understand?" he said.

"No."

"You will be taken off this mission and given a counseling

statement. You can go through your Chain of Command. I will give you an Article 15 if you do not remove your rank. I am tired of giving you orders."

"You've only given me one, sir."

"Why do you challenge everything?" Pugh asked, shaking his head.

The CO interjected. "You are driving us crazy, Specialist Ter-rez. You need to take off E-5 and put on E-4 until you have a ceremony."

"Kiester and Worrel," I said evenly, "didn't get a ceremony. They were just given their paperwork. And Shaves bought his own rank after he received his orders."

"It isn't your job to go around asking people anything." He looked my uniform over. "You need to get a name tag."

During the war, I'd removed my name tag, rank, and branch of service, in the event I was captured by the enemy.

"There were five typos in your promotion. We have to call to question them," said the lieutenant.

I knew what he was referring to. I'd heard the rumors about the CO's nonsensical remarks: I was going to be hand-cuffed, and he was going to throw me in the brig for forging my orders. "They're signed by a lieutenant colonel. I wouldn't forge anything," I said.

"Orders have to be sent directly to me," said the CO.

I removed my rank and placed it in my BDU shirt pocket. If I couldn't wear my proper stripes, I wouldn't wear any. They left abruptly, and I went to my truck.

WHILE AT A STOP ON A MISSION in Kuwait a week later, Sergeant Horton, a white guy from North Carolina, was brushing my hair after I had finished washing it in my Kevlar helmet.

A Cut-Vee arrived, swirling sand in the air when it stopped. I could see the CO inside the front passenger seat and found his presence odd, since he hadn't been on missions.

He climbed out of the vehicle, making his way with quick strides in my direction. I wondered, *Now* what?

"Specialist Ter-rez?"

"Yes, sir." I moved quickly to put my hair up.

"No, that's not necessary. You're in the field. I'm here to promote you," he said curtly.

He pinned the rank on my lapel. "Congratulations." He raised his hand in a salute.

So did I.

As quickly as he had approached, he left.

Horton grinned from ear-to-ear. "Well, that's great. Congratulations, Sergeant Ter-rez."

"Thank you. It's the best promotion I've ever gotten. He couldn't do anything to stop it."

Although I was content with my stripes, I didn't let my guard down, and it was a good thing I hadn't. Lieutenant Colonel Oliver North never responded. I knew the letter had to have been intercepted. It's one of those feelings when you know that you know. I wondered what else was being concocted against me.

It was bad enough my truck license had been pulled when Burns, who was my ground-guide at the time, backed me right into the front of another truck. Although it had been his fault and he took responsibility for it, I had been taken off the road and had to retake the written portion of the test. It seemed I had even more enemies than I thought.

I wasn't going to be broken down, but I didn't know how much more animosity I could take without doing something to someone.

But I wouldn't have to wonder for much longer. Matters later reached their peak, leading me to attempt the unthinkable.

## 22

# Swept Under the Rug

YOU'RE ON THE SHIT LIST." Trost turned to face me from behind the steering wheel of our tractor-trailer. Through eyeglass lenses, his small focused eyes met mine.

"I know, but nobody has the balls to say anything. They're weak."

"They're afraid of the CO. Torres, they're not you."

"Higher ranks are supposed to lead by example."

"Yes, but they often don't."

"Too bad."

"You're right, but that's life. There's nothing you can do."

I stared at him, adamant. "Yes, there is. And I won't stop 'til somebody listens. I don't care how many fuckin' times I gotta say it."

"I know you don't. You're a strong woman."

"It's got nothing to do with that, Trost." I shook my head.

"They gotta cut the bullshit. You know, when I was in Kuwait, Horton was brushing my hair and a senior NCO asked him if something was going on. Horton says they get upset when they see me with anyone," I sneered. "...Like I'm somebody's property...backward-thinking idiots."

"I know what you mean. I don't know how many guys have asked me if *I've* gotten some off you."

"You see?" I scoffed. "Fuckin' dirtbags."

That conversation ended with the fact that my uphill battle would continue.

Not surprisingly, just when I was getting acclimated to running missions with Trost, the CO had me moved again—except this time to the maintenance platoon. I suppose he presumed I knew nothing about light-wheeled vehicle mechanics; I'd show them all.

Sergeant First Class Ressem, my new platoon sergeant, was professional, fair, and not steered by faulty leadership. It was no wonder that I never had any issues with the soldiers in that platoon.

Standard-on-the-Job-Training was offered for the Heavy-Wheeled Vehicle Mechanics MOS. I approached Ressem one afternoon in the blazing sun, wearing my zippered sand-colored monkey suit, desert-camo floppy hat, and combat boots. He was standing near a truck, smoking a cigarette, while a couple of soldiers worked on some vehicles.

"Sergeant Ressem?"

"Yes, Sergeant Torres?"

"I'd like to do SOJT to get an additional MOS. Is that possible?"

His dark, noble cerulean eyes rested on mine. "Sure, Sergeant Torres."

"When can I begin?"

"You can start working with Sergeant Hunter tomorrow."

A private tossed a bottle of water to one of the specialists entering the makeshift pool, a tarp inside a three-foot ditch held down by sandbags. It was where I had spent my twenty-fourth birthday that April—the second best gift I'd received—clad in shorts and t-shirt. The greatest present had been a bottle of alcohol Lopez had fermented in the desert, which I shared with my buddies.

"He'll train and supervise you at the same time. Once done, you'll be tested, and upon successful completion, you'll be awarded your new MOS."

"Great, thank you."

"You're welcome, Sergeant Torres."

Three weeks later, I received my additional MOS, obliterating any doubts about my capabilities.

One early evening while performing maintenance on a truck, I saw Ross crossing the motor pool towards me, head downcast, hands in his pockets, steps slower than usual. He looked up at me. "Sista, you done?"

I saw sorrow in his eyes, heard sadness in his voice. "I am now." After wiping my hands on a rag, I jumped off the truck, and asked, "You wanna go for a walk?"

He nodded. "Yeah, sista, that sounds good."

Leaving behind shirtless mechanics changing tires, we walked in silence through the hot, windless desert, stopping at the farthest trailer but still inside the wire. "Wanna get in the shade?" I asked.

"Yeah."

We sat underneath it, and there, with tears in his eyes, Ross removed a sheet of paper from his cargo pocket. He confided, "Sista, look, Rides give me this," and handed me a Red Cross telegram.

As I read the letter our platoon sergeant had handed him about his father's death, he whispered, "I don't wanna go home, sista."

Tenderly, I said, "You have to, Ross. It's family."

Shaking his head, he offered the only explanation he knew at that moment. "You, Burns, and Lo-peyz—you're my family now."

"That's your *dad*, Ross."

"I feel bad leaving all of you behind, especially you. You're my sista."

"Ross, you're gonna feel guilty not seeing your dad ever again. We're gonna be fine. Don't worry about us." But the brother I had grown to love in a short time still seemed to be struggling.

An idea came to me that would make him feel better. "How about we write each other? And I'll tell Rides to take me with him to the airport the day you leave."

A spark returned to his dark brown eyes. He smiled and replied, "Okay, sista. That's a good i-dea. I like dat." He paused before saying, "I love yeu, sista."

"I love you, too, brother. I'm gonna miss you." We crawled out from beneath the trailer and strolled confidently to our hootch, arms over one another.

We kept our word. The closing of his letters were precious: *I am closing this letter, but not our friendship.* That was sweet ole Ross who'd remain in Fort Eustis until we returned.

A few days later the pendulum of rumors to return home stopped. Lieutenant Colonel Banks had come from Battalion to hold a redeployment meeting at our company. I wasn't going to believe much of what was said; he was not a man of his word. He'd never gotten back to me with the JAG appointment he'd promised.

Although Banks had considered the CO's treatment of me a "personal vendetta" and claimed a three-star general was reviewing my case, I knew the situation would be swept under the rug.

However, the opposite was true in the civilian sector. Mom had received a letter from a lieutenant colonel advising her that my case was closed, but New Jersey's Senator Frank Lautenberg had asked for further investigation. My sister had also received mail from Senator Mack in Florida, who asked her to follow up at the end of May.

As the Battalion puppet uttered nonsense, I tuned out, recalling some distressing news Burns had shared the previous evening. "Daddy told me some sick stuff."

"What kind of sick stuff?" I'd asked.

"Minorities were fighting this war," he had said as we filled our canteens at the water bladder.

"What are you talking about?"

"He was watching CNN. They said the Pentagon had estimated lots of deaths. They wanted minorities killed to give whites more opportunity to raise America's economy. Troops were wanted in early, so the casualty rate would be higher."

"*That* was on the *news*?" I asked in disbelief.

"Yes. Daddy heard it."

"Is that why there are so many units here with minorities?" I asked, putting the cap on.

"Well, it makes sense. Don't it?"

"Yeah, but, Buddy, I don't wanna have to believe that's true. It'd be awful," I added, looking at the sand beneath my feet in discontent.

"It didn't happen that way. Daddy said Powell and Schwarzkopf went against it. They had the air strike first. Then they sent the ground troops in. They didn't want another Vietnam."

Five words brought me back to the redeployment meeting: "*Congratulations. You'll be home soon,*" Banks had said.

My pretentious CO had the nerve to stand there, expression arrogant, chest puffed out like a giant as if he'd done a good job as commander. I looked up and scoffed, daggers in my eyes. I couldn't stand the man. I was seething, my head filling with rage as I recalled his denial when I requested to see a chaplain. He'd ordered me on a friendly mission instead, exploiting the essence of God as if He could be mocked. I eventually did it on my own anyway, knowing completely well a soldier's request to see one could not be denied.

I couldn't stand the hypocrisy and zoned out again, playing a recent radio broadcast in my head: "The armed services are an equal opportunity employer." It was laughable. "Minority only means less in number." I wished everyone would abide by that.

Specialist Laight's comments one afternoon earlier in the week provoked my thoughts further. In order to disclose the truth to the public, some of the women from Galax had written to the local paper, informing them of the gross manner in which the female soldiers had been treated.

Laight had entered the tent, furious, venting at no one in particular. "Can you believe the newspaper never printed our letter? The editor said it was degrading to the CO."

"I believe it. They're afraid to stand up," I'd said, looking over from the weapons course book spread out before me while lying on my cot.

"But that's not right—" She'd stopped herself. "Ter-rez, I have to tell you what Mudd said."

"What?"

"He said, 'Ter-rez came to this company and thought she could get with anyone she wanted, and look who she ended up with—Lester Burns. Well you can't blame Burns. I wouldn't fuck a nigger either.'"

"You sound just like him. You must've remembered every word," I said, matter-of-factly.

"I wrote down all the comments and racial slurs that were said while I was in third platoon's tent. The sergeants harassed *me*, too. Wilbur and Shug made passes and propositioned me."

At the sound of Wilbur's name, Sergeant Sara had looked up from her cot; she'd been wiping her tattered boots with a damp rag. "Wilbur said he'd take *care* of me if I'd go to bed with him."

"That's gross," Laight had said .

We'd laughed, seconding her remark, adding our own derogatory ones.

Flems had jumped in, leaping, boots thumping on the ground. "I hate that fucker. He made a mess of this company."

"Who?" Manning, waking from her nap, had asked, pushing the green camouflage liner she used as a privacy curtain to the side.

"The CO," replied Flems.

"Well, you ain't the only one, darling." Manning had sat up on her cot.

Perhaps it would've been better to put the women in the same tent from the start; we hadn't been able to share stories or build camaraderie.

"How about we light up his tent?" Flems had flicked her cigarette lighter on, raising her eyebrows in excited repetition, eyes cartwheeling in glee.

"That lighter's not gonna do it," I said, unmoved.

"Aw, shit, Ter-rez." Flems had stomped her foot, ashen face replaced by rosy cheeks.

"But it wouldn't be a bad idea if it did," I had added.

Finding my comment encouraging, she'd exclaimed, "Hell, you got that right! I think lots of these troops here would agree."

"I do too," Manning had said.

The movement of soldiers on their feet in that redeployment meeting brought me back to the present; it was my cue that it had ended. I headed to my tent to sleep, welcoming my day off from maintenance, wondering how it would all end.

# 23

# Madness

EVERYBODY HAS A BREAKING POINT. Mine began in the middle of a warm, dark evening as my fan oscillated. It was a few nights after Laight heard me shout in my sleep: "I think it's time." It seemed to have been an omen.

Lying on my cot, unable to sleep, I began thinking and thinking. Pictures of all the personal abuse I had endured due to an ignorant, self-absorbed CO kept flashing through my head, each repetition taunting me further. It could've all been prevented. I shouldn't have been the one to attempt to resolve matters.

*I'm a squared-away soldier. Why won't he stop? Is he getting a kick out of this?*

As thoughts continued to multiply in my head, faster with every passing second, a controlled anger burned. I came up with a plan.

I decided he deserved to die. I'd kill him myself, preferring to risk getting caught rather than continue to deal with him, his lack of civility and glorified perception of himself.

Some would thank me—there was no question that I believed I was doing every sensible soldier a favor. In fact, perhaps that was why he hadn't been on missions with us; had we been in a firefight, he might've been a casualty: excessive bullet holes caused by traveling rounds or accidentally hitting the wrong target. I can't say that some of my ammo wouldn't have been depleted, nor would I have blamed or given up anyone else whose ammo had.

I was determined.

Waiting until everyone was sound asleep, I put on the long burgundy robe that I had bought at the Saudi mall. It had two deep pockets on the front; the right one contained my best knife.

Our rifles, grenades, and ammunition were long gone; the cease-fire had ensured all had been turned in. I held onto the smooth blade, and the feel of it kept my objective in mind. In order to not reveal my position, I left my flashlight behind on that moonless night.

Standing barefoot at my tent entrance, I waited for my eyes to adjust to the dark, then headed slowly to his tent, the farthest one away, where he and Fifer slept. It wasn't my intention to kill the first sergeant; he had simply been spineless. However, if he woke up to see me, I'd have had to make a momentary decision.

The night was still, air clear, roving guard nowhere near me. As I headed to my destination, breathing quietly, I noticed a light coming from my old hootch in second platoon.

Would my plan be thwarted? I wondered.

I entered the tent to find McGirt playing cards with Dalton, a white guy from North Carolina; both were smoking cigarettes.

Keeping my hands in my pockets, I asked, "What's up, guys? What are you doing up?"

"Oh," said Dalton, "McGirt couldn't sleep. He saw a spider."

I laughed. "Get outta here McGirt, a camel spider? Come on!"

Dalton shook his head, bright blue eyes displaying the truth before he spoke. "No, Te-rez. He's deathly afraid of them."

"Yeah," McGirt admitted. "I'm scared of those things," he confessed.

"You're kidding, right?" I asked him.

"No, I'm serious. I can't sleep knowing they could be close by," he shivered, scattering the accumulated ashes of his cigarette to the ground.

"Yeah," Dalton agreed, letting out a puff. "I was still awake and said I'd keep him company."

Suddenly, Wratt, my former platoon sergeant, walked in. With uncertain accusation in his tone, he asked, "Te-rez, what are you doing here?" Wratt's pathetic nervousness was laughable—twitching nose and exaggerated gum chewing caused his prescription glasses to rise and fall.

I gripped the handle of my knife tight. "I couldn't sleep and went for a walk, then I saw their light on."

"Well, you need to leave now. You know females are not allowed in male tents anymore."

No one said anything.

"Come on. I'll walk you back to your tent."

"Bye, guys," I said.

McGirt spoke first. "Bye, Torres."

"See ya, Te-rez," echoed Dalton.

Little did the platoon sergeant know that he had just saved two lives: the CO's and mine. I knew that, no matter how well I hid that knife in the vast desert, it would've been found. Indeed, God had used my own enemies to protect me.

A few weeks later, a newfound discovery added more deception to certain members of the 4-2-4.

"Torres, you under there?"

I heard Burns' voice and slid out on a four-wheeled wooden board from beneath a truck. "What's up, Buddy?"

"Sergeant Scarlet wants to speak to you when you're done." Scarlet was a quiet, respectful black sergeant from North Carolina.

"About what?" I asked, squinting in the sun behind Buddy's head.

His voice dropped a notch. "Torres, it's sensitive. When will you be done?"

"I'm almost done—a few minutes, and then I just gotta put gook on my hands. You wanna wait?"

"Okay."

Once I was finished, Buddy said very little on the walk over. Troops were hanging around, and he didn't want to be overheard.

An apprehensive Scarlet stood near the male latrines.

"Hey, Scarlet, she's here."

"Thanks, Burns. Thank you for coming, Ter-rez," he said.

"What's going on?" I asked as we stepped away from the latrines.

"Around June 6, when I was sleeping in my tent, I heard a hammering noise. It woke me up, and I went to see what it was. I saw Tapirs and Earl in a connex, making a wooden box. Next to the box were all kinds of weapons. They had some tools, too. The XO, Lieutenant Pugh, was telling them what to do."

At that time, any weapons and souvenirs acquired had already been collected, burnt in a pile. "What connex number?" I asked.

"Nine."

"And then what happened?"

"They put the box under the water bladder with the weapons inside it."

Burns explained, "The water bladder weighs about six thousand pounds. MPs don't check underneath it when sealing a connex for shipment to the U.S., because it's too heavy to lift."

I nodded and turned to Scarlet. "You saw them doing all that?"

"Yes—the lieutenant was holding a light and giving them orders, but when he saw me, he turned it off. Then he asked me what I wanted. I said nothing, and then he told me to go back in the tent, so I did."

"What do you want me to do?"

"I want you to report it when you get home."

"Why don't you do it?"

"I'm afraid they'll find out it was me, and I don't want to do it here for the same reason. It's easier for you because you're from another state."

Scarlet had made complaints about some members of his platoon, and they had been discovered. "Okay. Give me a written statement."

"Can I give it to you the day before we go home?"

It was obvious to me that he was paranoid. "Yeah, sure."

Smuggling weapons was a serious crime, and Burns and I exchanged glances, anticipating something finally being done in that "ate-up"—as some troops called it—company.

"Thanks, Ter-rez."

"No problem, Scarlet. You're one of the good guys. I'll go to CID in Fort Dix when I return."

"Criminal Investigation Division, right?" asked Scarlet.

"Yeah," I said.

When Buddy and I broke off, he said, "See, in the end you'll win."

"It was never about that. I just wanted to be left alone to do my job."

AMID AROMAS OF MEAT LOAF and mashed potatoes in the dimly lit mess tent one evening about a week later, I was sitting on a picnic table across from Burns and Lopez, talking about everything and anything, when Manning entered.

"Hi." She came to a stop at the edge of our table. "Did you all hear?" she asked, holding a lit cigarette in her right hand, wriggling the fingers of the other in anticipation.

"What now?" I asked.

"We're going home!" Her sky blue eyes sparkled with hope despite the enmity she had against the CO.

"Yeah, right, for the fifteenth time this week. The worst

thing they did was name that meeting 'redeployment'. People actually believed it," I concluded with a note of sarcasm.

Burns chuckled, "Uh-huh."

Lopez smirked, raising his thick dark eyebrows in suspicion.

"It's true this time." She took a puff and let it out, adding, "It came from higher up."

"Where'd you hear it?" asked Lopez.

"This morning in the headquarters meeting."

"Oh. I guess it *is* true," I said apathetically.

"We'll all be home by the Fourth of July. I can't wait. The first thing I'm going to do is get out of this unit," said Manning.

"That's right. That's the first thing you should do," agreed Lopez.

"Well, I'm out of this ignorant company too, and a whole lotta other troops. I don't know if he'll have anyone to make hell for." Burns' chuckled and clapped his hands, causing his shoulders to rise and fall.

In between drags, Manning added, "You're right, Burns. I'm just glad it's all over. He's made my life here hell."

"Yeah, he has. Pulling your rank and giving it back to you like it was a yo-yo, and sending the First Sergeant to see if you'd 'get with him,'" I scoffed. "He's disgusting, and he's married, too. I guess he thinks adultery in the UCMJ doesn't apply to him. Fuckin' asshole thinks he can lead. Listen, girl, don't get me going."

Manning, ever graceful, suggested, "We have to spend some time together when we get home. You all can come visit me."

"I definitely will," I said.

"I'll be there, too. If my wife's spent all my money, I won't have a home to go to," said Burns matter-of-factly.

"I'm going to spend some time with my sons. After that, I don't know," said Lopez in a flat tone.

"Manning, does McGirt know?" I asked.

"I haven't told him."

"You should. The CO's been on him, too. McGirt's made complaints to Battalion."

"I'll go with you to tell him," offered Lopez.

Watching them leave, I asked myself what home was. Leaning forward, elbows on knees, chin resting on one palm, I asked, "Buddy, how do you really feel about going home?"

"I don't know, Torres."

"Me neither. . .is that normal?"

"I don't know."

"So what do we know?"

"Well, besides not getting the money, nothing." The king of Saudi Arabia had wanted to thank each troop with a gift of ten thousand dollars for a job well done.

I chuckled. "Yep. Bush said we weren't paid mercenaries. Too bad—it would've been nice."

"Yeah, it sure would have."

"So what do we do? I mean, what happens after this?"

"Torres, I know exactly what you know. I guess we all have to take it one day at a time."

I twirled my fingers around the table's creases and looked up. "I don't like that."

"Well, why not, if that's all we can do?"

"Because I don't know if it'll fill the void."

"What void?"

"The not knowing, the danger, the bullshit, the staying on your toes. You know, *that*."

He rubbed his hands together, nodding his head as he eyed me with confirmation. "You'll get it."

"How do you know?"

"Because you won't stop until you do."

# 24

# Aftermath

WELL, WE'RE ALL DONE PACKING and disassembling the tents. We'll be in Khobar, right where we started. Looks like we'll be home soon," Burns said, sitting across from me on the sand after an MRE dinner. "Can I tell you something?" he asked.

"Of course."

"I had a dream about you in Eustis."

"A dream? About me?"

"Yeah, before you got to Eustis. It's almost like I knew you were coming, but I didn't know why."

I leaned forward. "And?"

"I saw you in my dream, and I felt like God was saying, 'You see that one? Take care of her. Don't let anything happen to her.'"

I nodded. "I could see why He said that. You did a good

job, Buddy. You even walked away from the first sergeant when he tried to get you to stop talking to me by bribing you with an E-6 promotion."

"Uh-huh, that's right. Well, who wants a promotion that way?"

"So, why'd you give me a hard time when I wanted to be friends?"

He shrugged. "I guess I just wanted to make sure it was you. And when you kept following me around, being a pest, I said, 'Goodness gracious. Lord, you sure? That little mouth of hers cuts people up big.' I didn't think you'd be so feisty."

I laughed loudly before remarking, "Well, I had to defend myself. What else you expect me to do when people give me a hard time? Take it?"

"No, you did the right thing, and you kept me from going off on these whatchacall ate-up men. You're a strong female," he replied.

"Thanks. . .you know, God gave you the gift of seeing things. I still remember what you told me when we first got to Khobar."

"What?"

"You said you had a vision that I was on a stage."

"Yeah, uh-huh. You were standing up on stage talking on the microphone and a whole lot of people were on the ground listening to you."

"You remember what I said?"

He started laughing. "Yes, good gosh, the devil thing."

"It's okay to say 'hell,' Buddy, it's a real word, not a curse word. It's in the dictionary." I shook my head. "So what'd I say?"

"You said you didn't know what the hell you'd be talking about but you believed me. Torres. . .you'll be alright wherever you go."

DURING REDEPLOYMENT AT KHOBAR, an army investigator from Washington, DC, came to see me to look into my sexual harassment claims. Captain French maintained a poker face as I spoke.

Once done, he rose, ironing out his desert camouflage uniform, and in a slow nasal tone said, "I'll pick you up tomorrow morning. You can use my office typewriter to put it all on paper."

During the days that followed, French interviewed the chain of command and about thirty-five troops. My superiors spoke well of my soldier skills, except for Wratt, who said I'd been in second platoon's tent when it was off limits to the females but added that I'd followed orders when told to leave. The troops all testified that I had been sexually harassed.

French called me into his office after the investigation's completion. "Sergeant Torres, I will submit my report for a determination. You may write your congressman to obtain the results when you return home."

"That's it, sir?"

"Yes, Sergeant."

Hurry up and wait, I thought. It's the typical military way.

A few days later, wearing new desert uniforms, we boarded a military plane towards Andrews Air Force Base in Virginia. The ride felt lighter, quicker.

Before you knew it, we had landed in America and marched

down the aircraft's steps to an incredible sight: hundreds of friends and families wearing yellow ribbons, waving American flags, cheering loudly while the press snapped photographs.

From afar, I saw Mom and Marissa carrying balloons and flowers, smiles bright. As I neared them, tears rolled down their faces, eyes expressing relief. Hugs lingered upon embracing.

Then the sight was grander: Ross was strutting between the crowds, grinning from ear to ear.

"Brother!" I jumped with joy, shouting for Burns and Lopez, who were farther away.

"Hey, sista—I told you I'd be here!" he exclaimed, just as proud as the father who sees his baby girl for the first time.

The company was given some free time, and our group went to dine at Red Lobster, which felt surreal. Afterward, the guys and I returned to the barracks. Mom and Marissa went back to New Jersey.

Morning exit physicals brought questions about environmental exposures, psychological stressors, and other medical issues. I documented my exposure to large quantities of dust, sand, and smoke, and recorded taking over twenty-one PBs.

We were ordered to answer "no" to the question: *Do you have any reason to believe that you, or any members of your unit, were exposed to chemical warfare or germ warfare?* I did as instructed.

Soon afterward, it was time to return home. My brother Ross promised to stay connected.

Lopez and I had rented a car to drive back together. Before we parted ways with Burns, the three of us looked at one other.

"See you in ten years," I said, reading their eyes. We felt that the U.S. would return to the Gulf in due time because

Hussein had not been killed. In addition, we felt that the enemy would be more astute, having gained better knowledge of American fighting tactics.

Burns left to North Carolina, and to this day he remains my buddy. The young kids he had then are now grown, and he is a grandpa. His marriage, however, didn't last. In 2010, he remarried, and four years later, he retired from the highway patrol.

Lopez and I saw each other once during a chance encounter when McGirt and I were in Fort Totten.

In 1993, Trost, McGirt, and his fiancée Gloria came to a party I threw. Later, I went to McGirt's wedding in Brooklyn, but I haven't seen him since.

Trost and I are still in touch; we have visited each other throughout the years. He went back to school, got an engineering degree, attended Officers Candidate School, and is now a retired captain. He lives in Rochester, New York, with his wife and teenage son, and has a daughter in college.

Ross and I wrote for many years. He visited me in New Jersey in the fall of 2000. But sadly, my dear brother and I also lost contact.

Manning is retired from the Army. We see one another on occasion.

In August 1991, I spent a day with Brown and McMillian in Virginia. We lost touch but reconnected many years later. Today, Brown is a preacher, and McMillian is a businessman.

Back home on the third of July, I felt out of place in a life that appeared mundane. I wondered what I was expecting to accomplish in that mediocre existence.

Rose and Marissa invited me to watch the fireworks display over the magnificent New York City skyline from Boulevard East in West New York. I wasn't my usual talkative self.

The night was warm, but having become accustomed to the desert heat, I was shivering in a blazer and pants. From the front passenger seat, random popping sounds outside brought me anxiety. I'd stiffen as people walked haphazardly through the streets to stand near strangers. I wondered if I'd be able to do that.

Someone passed too close to the car, and I ducked. "I don't like this," I said to Rose. Then I heard a whistle. "Get me outta here now."

"Okay," she said, easing the car around the block.

At home, I lay down on the bed, covering my ears with pillows while the sound of thunderous fireworks echoed in my head.

For many years thereafter, I remained indoors on the Fourth of July.

That wasn't the only change. Insignificant things like an unexpected gesture or a negative comment about the armed forces made me combative.

Military movies were another matter. They brought me back to the Gulf, where memories of my maltreatment would fuel my rage. This led me to avoid them.

People on the road annoyed me, whether they moved too slowly, used inappropriate signals, or rode their brakes. Anger would consume me in an instant. I'd speed up, tailgate, honk my horn, and use many expletives, always ready to fight. I knew I'd have to wait it out like every other soldier and hoped I could control my reactions.

Sensing detachment from my friends and family, I telephoned Burns and Manning, whose experiences were not dissimilar. We decided to meet in Virginia.

There in the comfort of each other's presence, we agreed that life as we had known it had dramatically changed. Knowing we could not remain with one another indefinitely made us question what would happen to us. We separated with the understanding that we knew very little.

One day at home that week, on my way to the shower, Mom was cooking. Without preface, I said, "Ma, put the knives away and don't tell me where they are."

She stopped stirring the spoon but said nothing.

"Another thing, Ma—when I'm sleeping, don't wake me up suddenly by shouting. Just whisper."

Continual nightmares had plagued me since my return. The same tall, thin man with the dark hair and penetrating eyes chased but never caught me. Each dream pattern was sequential; warfare skills and locations became more complicated.

Falling asleep was something I tried to avoid, but sleep deprivation would've triggered other issues. Yet no matter when I fell asleep, the man wearing black resurfaced. I'd try to remove myself from the nightmare but couldn't. It'd seem something was weighing me down. During those times, my assailant continued to taunt me.

Upon awakening, my heart would be beating faster and I'd be sweaty, edgy, or wiped out. However, as odd as it may sound, many times I yearned to be back in the Gulf, where it'd seemed that life had more meaning.

I understand why some soldiers don't want to return home and end up volunteering for more tours. Had the Gulf War not ended, I would've stayed on with another unit.

One morning soon after, when I awoke, I noticed Mom's heavy floral vase on the floor at my bedside. Putting it on the dresser where it belonged, I walked to the kitchen.

She looked up from the bowl of cereal she was having but said nothing, something she had gotten into the habit of doing—waiting for me to speak first.

"Ma, why was the vase on the floor?"

Her eyes widened. "Don't you remember?"

"Remember what?"

"You were sleepwalking."

"*What?* I don't do that." How could that be? I wondered.

"You did last night."

"What'd I do?"

"In the middle of the night, you sat up straight on the bed. You looked around the room, moved your eyes but not your head. Then you got up, walked to the dresser, lifted the vase, and placed it on the floor next to you. After that, you fell asleep."

"Good thing you put the knives away," I said, and entered the bathroom. In the absence of a weapon, my mind must've identified the vase as one.

Not remembering was troubling, but the worst part was the look of fear on her face. I would not hurt her, and I wondered if she now thought I would. Thankfully, that incident did not recur.

As time passed, the nightmares began to lessen, until they disappeared, and I thought I had been liberated.

ON AUGUST 1, I HEADED TO the Criminal Investigation Division in Fort Dix, turned over Scarlet's statement, and provided one myself. The special agent said that the connex would be inspected once it was stateside.

Months later, I learned through Manning that AK-47s had been found in connex number nine, but Pugh, upon being questioned, said they had been brought back for the museum. That was that. Pathetic.

The outcome of the sexual harassment complaints remained unsettled until mid-October. Two letters arrived from the Department of the Army, Office of the Inspector General, Washington, DC. Senator Lautenberg, of New Jersey, and Representative Mack, of Florida, concluded: *The allegation that Specialist Torres was sexually harassed by soldiers in her unit was substantiated. Appropriate action has been taken concerning those individuals involved.*

ON JUNE 28, 1995, REPRESENTATIVE ROBERT MENENDEZ sent me further findings from investigating officers: ". . .the allegation of harassment by fellow soldiers (peers) in her unit against SP4 Torres was substantiated. Acting IG and Bn Cdr basically ignored not only Torres' pleas for help, but the IG's attempts to speak with them concerning their lack of concern. SGT Torres had a group of soldiers that she was friends with and she tried to spend time with them. The entire chain of command talked during the interviews about hearing rumors about what was going on but said they couldn't act on rumors. I informed them that it was an entirely wrong answer. Her superiors, instead of helping her solve her problems, hindered her."

Better something than nothing. Although I believed appropriate action would not be taken against the perpetrators, reading that my claims had been substantiated brought me affirmation. At last, I felt vindicated.

# 25

# Fork in the Road

BEFORE MY MILITARY ORDERS ENDED on July 24, 1991, I tapped my employer's office door early one morning. "Chief?"

He looked up from his desk and rose. "Julia! I heard you were back. Welcome home."

"Thank you. May I come in?"

"Of course. Please, sit down." He pointed to a chair. "What can I do for you?"

"Chief, I've been experiencing things at a different level."

"Yes, I imagine you have."

"I don't want to continue doing what I did. Too boring. I want to be an investigator, and if you won't hire me, I want you to know I'm going elsewhere."

He chewed that over for a moment or two. "I know what you must've gone through overseas can't compare to the duties of your current position. However, the office policy requires. . ."

I tuned him out until the drone stopped. "Chief, that's not always the case. Consider this my resignation."

I stood up, and so did he. "Well, I'm sorry you feel that way." He offered his hand. "Good luck in your career."

Confident that someone would hire me, I submitted my resume to the other twenty-one county prosecutor's offices, honing in on the narcotics task forces. Though I was looking forward to a bright future, a previous conversation with Tadea, Marissa's older sister, resurfaced.

We had been at a friend's wedding reception in mid-July; our dates had gone to get bar drinks when she suddenly asked, "Julie, I know you think of this guy as a friend, but are you seeing someone?"

"No, I just got back from the Gulf, and honestly I can't be bothered. I know me. I'll jump into dead-end relationships, or if I really start to like the guy, or he mentions the 'L' word, I'll act like a bitch so he'll leave me."

"Why would you do that?"

I sighed. "Look, Tadea, I gotta have sex in the dark, or I gotta have a buzz."

She had frowned. "Julie, you have to stop. Every time you do that, he's doing it to you all over again."

I stared at her with a blank expression, knowing she had spoken the crude truth. The guys returned, and I welcomed the reprieve.

My rape would remain unaddressed for the next two years, and I continued to live as an emotional cripple. I knew it would turn up somehow, some way. I was simply buying time.

In the interim, I waited to see which agency would get back to me first until a week later, when Mom knocked on my bedroom door. "Aurorita, you have a letter from the court."

The remittance read *Sussex County Prosecutor's Office*, one of the least busy task forces. *Odd. . .of all places.* I contacted them and scheduled an interview.

After I met with an assistant prosecutor, a sergeant, the chief, and the prosecutor, things moved fast. I was hired as an investigator for the Narcotics Task Force, and the following week I was filling out paperwork at Personnel.

The next police class was going to begin in late August at the Division of Criminal Justice Police Academy in Lawrenceville, New Jersey. Until then, I read about drugs, asked colleagues lots of questions, moved to another area, and became familiar with Sussex County.

The absence of rampant crime in the vicinity made me wonder, though, where and how undercover work would fit in. It was rural; cows grazed in fields, and out-of-towners en-joyed hayrides and pumpkin picking at harvest. But I main-tained my focus—to complete the academy.

I'd become more performance-oriented, supplementing the trauma with accomplishments, awards, and recognition from other agencies. If my successes couldn't erase the cruelty I had gone through, at least they'd give me purpose.

Every day brought my police career closer—as well as the reality of being a narco, not a Hollywood version of it. I'd learn how to break doors, become more comfortable playing different undercover roles, and get craftier after every drug purchase.

It was no longer a death wish I craved but excitement, the thrill of the unexpected, the high of the danger. To me, that was living life fully, and I was going to get it. Burns had been right: I wouldn't stop until I did.

## Author's Note and Acknowledgements

Forget grammatically correct right now. Let's just talk.

This book began taking form sometime in 2010 in Southern Cal, when I met Jamie Quattrochi, a producer, director, and actor, who asked for a synopsis of one of the police cases I worked undercover in. He loved it and asked me to write a book.

Thank you, Jamie, for believing my story had worth.

The spiral started from there.

One day in Jersey, I was talking to Rolando Corujo, a high-school classmate of mine, when the subject of true stories came out. I mentioned what I had written, and he asked to see it. He loved it and introduced me to Dave Riccardi, a former Simon & Schuster publisher, who introduced me to T. Sean Herbert, a former CBS producer, who introduced me to his wife, Taryn Grimes, a former Broadway actress. Talk about a snowball effect.

Thank you, Dave, Sean, and Taryn, for your belief in my work, your suggestions in your respective mediums, and your time.

Thank you, Rolando, for the intros, for starting up my blog, for designing such an awesome book cover, enhancing the photos, and for suggesting our high-school classmate, Mari, Maria Arriola-Fernandez, as editor.

Thank you, Mari, for your painstaking editing hours, your patience and thoroughness. Even when I wanted things done yesterday, you would not waver.

There was no way I could've planned this better; I knew God was behind it all. I'm just a Union City kid from down the block, I kept thinking. It was humbling to know that people of such caliber were interested in my life, but then again, nothing is impossible with God.

I met another person who'd be important in the development of this book through Jane Chagaris-Albanese. While at a women's retreat with Rutherford, New Jersey's, Abundant Grace Christian Church, Jane introduced herself, stating she heard I was writing a book and she was also. She recommended I attend writing seminars with Barry Sheinkopf, a published author involved with Full Court Press, a self-publishing company.

Thanks to Jane's referral of Barry, my once expository writing book developed into one immersed with dialog and the five triggers, something I had no idea of. Thank you, Barry, for your expertise and patience in teaching me the value of writing.

But it didn't end there; I continued writing, and to my surprise, my best friend Burns called me one night to say that Dr. Maya Angelou wanted to read two of my chapters. *The* Dr. Maya Angelou? I asked; I didn't know he knew her. Turned out he knew her administrative assistant, Patricia Casey, and had been sharing tidbits of my book with her. I want to thank Casey for believing my story must be told, for sharing it with Dr. Angelou, and for taking time from her personal life to edit many chapters in this book.

Anyway, based on Dr. Angelou's traumatic experiences, I figured she'd want to see if I'd be real with mine, so I sent her "Wolf in Sheep's Clothing" and "Demons To Bind"; she liked them. What an honor it was to know that her eyes had read my words, and that the possibility of her writing a blurb would exist! I was beside myself and, although I felt her death would occur before my book ended, sharing that part of my story with her was enough.

By the time my book was complete, it was about 700 pages—yeah 700; oh, and we conducted some interviews, too. Rolando suggested we record opinions from key people in my book in the event we'd ever do an interactive book. That's Rolando, thinking technology.

I'd like to thank those of you who agreed to the use of your real names, to be recorded with video, and answer unscripted questions. Others wished to remain private, but they shared moments of recollection, and I thank you also.

Many thanks go to my friends and family, who have supported me throughout this endeavor; those who waited patiently for it to be completed, and those who respected the time I spent in my cave to get this done.

Obviously *this* book isn't 700 pages long; I decided to end it here and begin the next with my career in law enforcement. It made sense to me. Otherwise, it was TMI.

I thought maybe some people would like the cop stuff better than the army stuff, or vice versa, and it really wasn't about either. It was about my rape, my behavior because of it, and what the lack of support caused to happen. I wanted victims to know they were, and are, not alone in their thinking or their actions, nor are they to ever blame themselves for what occurred. A crime is a crime!

Yes, there are still unanswered questions. They'll be revealed in the next book. I wrote this the way things developed in my life, and I didn't begin to address some issues until later, but that's just the way life is—so bear with me.

At this time, I'd like to thank you for reading my book and I sincerely hope that you feel better after having read it and that you have gained insight to help you or someone else heal. That's what it's all about—healing.

Please do me one favor. As you know, I learned about God's love for me when I was thirteen; I asked for forgiveness, accepted His gift of Jesus, and allowed Him to enter my heart. However, although I knew the Holy Spirit was the one Christ left behind to console us, I seldom if ever sought help. God was on the back burner; I hardly thanked Him for my successes nor did I, aside from surface prayer, really pray to Jesus. It would've been easier if I had shared my traumatic experiences. Don't be like me and wait. Tell Him everything.

I don't want it to be any harder for you or anyone you know who has been a victim of any crime. Please take this moment to seek God, whether you talk to Him aloud or through your mind, tell Him you believe He sent His son Jesus to die for you. Accept His gift of everlasting life through Christ. Ask Him for forgiveness; He knows we are not perfect. You'll see the peace you'll start to feel once you know God is in control of your life. And, you'll find that with the Holy Spirit who Jesus left behind for your consolation, you will never be alone. All you have to do is believe and ask. It's really that simple.

—J.T.

*New York Metropolitan Area, December 2014*

RESOURCES

God: 24/7 Prayer Line
Agent Orange Helpline 1-800-749-8387
Center for Minority Veterans 1-202-461-6191
Equal Rights Advocates 1-800-839-4372
Gulf War Helpline 1-800-749-8387
Homeless Veterans 1-877-424-3838
National Alliance of Families for the Return of
America's Missing Servicemen 406-652-3528
and 718-846-4350
National Center for Posttraumatic Stress Disorder
(PTSD) 802-296-6300
National Sexual Assault Hotline 800-656-HOPE
(4673)
Returning OEF/OIF/OND Service Members
877-222-8387
Survivor Benefits 800-827-1000
Veterans Crisis Line 800-273-8255 Press "1"
Women Veterans Health Care 855-829-6636

*Credits:*
http://www.militaryeducation.org/10-most-epic-
tank-battles-in-military-history/
http://www.nytimes.com/1991/02/26/world/war
-in-the-gulf-scud-attack-scud-missile-hits-a-
us-barracks-killing-27.html
http://www.poetpatriot.com/timeline/tmwar-
gulf.htm

## ABOUT THE AUTHOR

Julia Torres believes one never stops learning. By the age of twenty-seven, she had obtained a bachelor of arts degree and a teacher certification, enlisted in the U.S. Army, become a Veteran of the Persian Gulf War, and graduated from a New Jersey police academy. In law enforcement, she worked undercover for local, county, state, and federal agencies.

In 2001, after a diagnosis of multiple sclerosis, Torres, then a single parent of a toddler, retired from law enforcement, but that didn't stop her. She devoted her time to raising a strong, confident child, and volunteered at police departments and courthouses to assist adults and children, victims of crime. Later, she became involved in acting and attended Bible studies. Currently, she is preparing the way for her daughter's future in college, while working on two degrees, a Masters in Homeland Security, and a Bachelors in Ministry. Her future husband, she believes, is right around the corner.

"You intended to harm me, but God intended it for good to accomplish what is now being done, the saving of many lives."

—*Genesis* 50:20 (NIV)

Continue reading
for a sneak preview
of the sequel to this book,

# Bolder and Braver
*My Undercover Life*

# *I*

# Methods of Instruction

POLICE FILMS ARE A GROSS EXAGGERATION of the intricacy of law enforcement, not to mention undercover work." Using his hands to make his points, our instructor paced back and forth. "Actors don't run out of ammo, and if they do, their weapon doesn't lock to the rear, they just keep shootin'. I'd like to have that gun."

The other cadets and I loved listening to a professor who taught with a sense of humor. At nine o'clock in the morning, Vito Palumbo made it seem as if lunchtime was in the next five minutes.

"They don't follow chain-of-evidence but check out what they do. They toss evidence around in the squad room like it's a ball. I'd like to see my boss walk in to find a bag in his face. We'll all be under investigation, without pay, too. We don't dodge bullets from high-powered rifles on a regular basis, or leap over tall buildings consecutively. Hell, I can't even jump one."

Laughter followed.

"And guys, the most important thing. . . ." Students leaned in closer, hanging on the last words the short Italian with an unsuspecting police presence spoke. "When it comes to conducting search warrants, don't follow their lead or you'll get killed."

Students sat up straight—the word *kill* has the tendency to do that, bring respect to it, thus changing the environment. That morning was no different as the reality of death hung in the air, but Palumbo moved on.

"Honestly, I never shot out of my car while in hot pursuit in the middle of the city. . .too many people, somebody's gonna get killed, the city's gonna get sued, and probably me, too. That's Hollywood."

A student raised his hand., "Sir, how often do you chase a suspect?"

"As an undercover?"

"Yes."

"I never have. That's not my job."

"What is?" someone called out.

"The UC walks the walk, talks the talk, and gathers information and evidence to make a solid case. Then he or she writes articulate reports. Surveillance teams can chase 'em."

"I have a surveillance question," I said.

"Okay, shoot."

"How close are the teams, and how much can they hear?"

"It depends how close they can get without being made, but just 'cause they're there doesn't mean they could hear shots fired."

Chairs screeched, and remarks were made.

"Why not?" asked a man seated in the rear.

"Murphy's Law."

Expletives followed.

"Okay, guys, look—it's great to have back-up, don't get me wrong, but the UC must always work thinking that he or she is alone. Use your personality, but remember you're acting. Don't lose yourself in the role. Be a good bullshitter, but know how to get out without getting killed."

"Do you always carry?" asked a young man.

"No."

The student muttered something under his breath.

"I know how you feel, but I can't always explain having one."

The instructor made his way to the center of the class, standing still as if for effect before glancing at everyone. "Guys, listen, what you learn here is *book* knowledge. It's what you need to know to get certified, but by no means is this the street. Let me ask you this. Would you take your gun to buy a dime bag from a street dealer, or to discuss bank transactions with a money launderer, or to place a bet with a bookie—or, better yet, if you're gonna be introduced to a wise guy?"

Some of my classmates nodded, and some shook their heads. Others shrugged.

Having made his point, his arms went up. "Exactly. See how you don't know? It all depends on the circumstances. In my opinion, it should be up to the undercover to make that decision, if experienced, or the supervisor, if not."

The invaluable lesson had been absorbed: I'd be alone,

armed or not. If I couldn't talk myself out of a situation, then undercover work was no longer for me.

Graduation came that December, and I beamed with pride at my police certification. There was nowhere to go but up, yet I knew it wouldn't be in Sussex.

It was lame. At that time, deep cover investigations meant wearing a hair net in a cookie factory where it was presumed there was narcotics activity. Luckily, employees smoking a joint outdoors during their lunch break did not fall into that category, and that job was short-lived.

As the months dragged by, I'd take compensatory time to break up the monotony. That May was no different when I flew to Miami Beach to stay with my sister Marlene and got in touch with Roman.

We'd met in March 1990 at a nightclub near the beach. Whenever I was in the area, we'd get together. Although we shared a mutual attraction, there hadn't been any intimacy. The bad habits I'd developed of having sex in the dark, with a buzz or not, had made me hesitant.

However, on May 13, 1992, the final night of that trip, after spending a fun-filled evening dancing at a beach club, I decided to spend the night with him. Before I fell asleep, I knew I had conceived.

About a week later in Jersey, I made an appointment to see an OB-GYN, who confirmed my pregnancy. Carrying the child of a stranger brought the realization that my negative behavior had to cease, but I was happy. . .he'd be someone to love wholly. There was no doubt in my mind that I'd give birth to a boy.

I boarded a flight to relay the news to Roman the following

month. I had no ulterior motives, no desire to marry him, nor any monies to demand. Simply, he had the right to know.

Roman's response was conflicted—supportive at first, then doubtful. Not appreciating his lack of character, I advised him not to contact me and returned home.

Work resumed, but I said nothing, opting instead for the first trimester to pass. Things took on a different turn in mid-June, when my sergeant sent me to a two-week DEA drug-training course in south Jersey.

I arrived early on the first day of class and was assigned to be the greeter. A twenty-something-year-old, olive-complexioned Filipino with high cheekbones entered. Notebook under an arm, Dunkin' Donuts coffee in a hand, he extended the other one out to me. "Hi, I'm Rick DeLeon. Nice to meet you." His smile was warm, noble.

"Julia Torres, but I'm the greeter, not you," I teased.

"Okay. Should we try this again?"

I laughed at his wit. "No, that's okay. Have a seat. Class will begin when everybody's here."

"You sure about that?"

"Don't shoot the messenger," I said, raising my hands.

His loud laughter resonated confidence as he strolled off.

When everyone was seated, I went to the available seat in the first row. There was Rick seated to my left.

Moments later, I accidentally dropped my pen. *He's gonna pick it up.*

"Here you go," he said.

"Thank you."

"You're welcome."

*He's gonna start a conversation.*

"What department are you?"

"Sussex County Prosecutor's, Narcotics. You?"

"Hudson County Prosecutor's, Narcotics."

"Cool! That's where I wanna work."

He drank some coffee before saying, "Put your resume in."

"I did."

"Really? And Hudson didn't call you?" He seemed puzzled.

"No. I took the first agency that did."

"I'm surprised. You're Spanish and female. Send it again."

"Yeah, I was too, for those very reasons. I'll try again after I get some experience."

"In *Sussex?*" he laughed, causing others to turn in our direction.

I shrugged. "At least I got the academy done."

"You're right. It's easier to get hired after that paper's in your hands. Saves departments time and money. That's smart. You live in Sussex?" he asked, finishing his coffee.

"You crazy?" I answered rhetorically, slapping his arm. "I live in Hudson."

He chuckled, "Easy, there. Remind me not to say that again. So where do you live?"

"Union City."

"Oh—I live in Jersey City. Greenville."

"We're neighbors."

"You wanna carpool?"

"Yeah, that'd be great," I said before the training instructor entered the room, filling it with his musky fragrance.

Commuting two hours each way gave Rick and me much

time to talk. My analysis of him began one afternoon on our drive back home as the radio played softly.

"You know, I like Filipinos."

"Really? Filipinos? Why is that?" he asked, taking a puff of his cigarette.

"I've had good experiences with them."

"Good how?" His small brown eyes expressed curiosity.

"Well, one of my best friends in high school was Filipino, and so was my pediatrician," I said, lowering the window, allowing the summer breeze to make cartwheels with my hair.

Bursting into laughter, he asked, "Your *pediatrician?*" He took another drag before flicking the ashes outside.

"Yeah. What's so funny? I saw him 'til I was twenty-three."

"Twenty-three? Are you crazy?"

"No. I was really comfortable with him."

"You don't say," he said in mockery.

I ignored his remark. "You know what ended it?"

"No. Tell me." He brought the cigarette to his lips.

"He said I had to see a real doctor."

"What?" his cigarette almost fell out when he snickered. "He *is* a real doctor."

"That's what I said, but he said I had to see a general practitioner, not him and I said, '. . .But, Doctor, I love you.'"

He roared. "You're crazy. You told the doctor you loved him?"

I shrugged, "Yeah, why not?"

Rick flicked his cigarette out the window. "So that's the reason you like Filipinos?"

"And because of my friend, too. Plus I really admire their

work ethic and how they're family oriented."

The more we spoke, the more I liked him as a person. During class, he listened attentively to others. When he was wrong, he did not mind being corrected.

In the mornings, he waited patiently when I made him wait to gauge his patience. He proved to be a man of detail when he sometimes surprised me with my favorite coffee and doughnut.

My comfort level led me to share the news of my pregnancy. I was glad I did; having a man's optimistic opinion was comforting.

My career began to unfold for the better one afternoon in class as we waited for the instructor. Surrounded by a smorgasbord of cologne, tenor whispers, and baritone laughter, I heard my name and turned.

"Hi. I'm Jon Tillwater."

Jon, a burly, blond six-footer with blue eyes, could've been a spectacular sports anchorman. His bass voice was clear and articulate.

"I'm a detective with the Lakewood Police Department, Special Operations Unit. We're conducting a narcotics operation this summer in a high drug trafficking area known as the Jungle. We're looking for undercover cops, and I think you'd be great. Would you be interested in coming on-loan?"

It was what I had been waiting for. "I'd love to!"

"Great. Let me have your sergeant's number, so we can speak with him."

The classroom instructor entered, and I quickly wrote my info on a piece of paper and handed it to Jon before the class began.

On one of our return trips, I brought up the subject of rape to test Rick. "You know, I have a friend that was date raped in college, and she had a hard time getting over it."

"Getting over it?" he asked, brows furrowed.

"Yeah. Why are you looking at me like that?"

"I don't know if those are the words I'd choose."

*Good man.* "What do you mean?"

"College date rapes are more common than people think, and just like rapes in general, they're highly unreported."

"Why?"

"Most reported rapes are made by adults who understand it for what it is. Don't get me wrong—some adults don't report them either, but they're not in the majority. Kids don't know what to do. Things like denial, shame, personal blame, accusations from others, you know, some of what we call Rape Trauma Syndrome, prevent them from going to the police."

"How do you know that?" I asked.

"I read a lot, and I paid attention in the academy."

*He's scoring big points.* "But why deny it?"

"It's easier to ignore the trauma than to address it."

"Makes sense," I nodded. "Why feel ashamed, then, if she did nothing wrong?"

"Assuming it's a she, maybe she drank a little too much, made out with him a little, and the guy didn't take no for an answer when she wanted him to stop."

I shook my head. "No, that wasn't it for my friend."

"Well, maybe your friend felt people would accuse her," he suggested.

"But why would someone do that?"

"It happens more often than people realize. Even the

mother sometimes blames the daughter."

"How could she? It's her own daughter."

"She might be an old school parent, maybe ignorant, maybe doesn't wanna deal with it. . .without even knowing, she's actually making it worse."

"So why not ask for advice?"

"Some parents find the whole ordeal shameful and don't want to acknowledge it. Some even tell the kids to keep quiet if they know the perp."

I was indignant. "But it's not about them! They'd rather have their own flesh and blood live in torment than tell the police?"

"Sometimes—but remember, if they're not acknowledging the rape, they're blind to their pain. The perp may, at times, live in the same home."

"That's horrible. There's no healing then."

"No, and that's why it's often repressed. Then people wonder why a rape victim snaps and kills someone years later. They should look at the root instead of asking how it could've been done."

"So how do they heal?"

"They start talking about it."

"To who?"

"A professional, a friend, someone who won't judge them."

"But what if they don't?"

". . .They have to start somewhere, Julia."

"That's a lot of heavy stuff to talk about." I turned to stare out the window.

"Yeah, but it should get done."

I had been content with his answers but didn't think it was the right time to disclose my rape. Instead, I said, "Working in that field must be tough. I don't know if I could do that."

"I'm sure you could."

I shook my head and grinned. "I don't think so. I'd have a hard time with the interrogation. I'd wanna hurt them."

"Some cops feel that way, but it makes them want to get a confession rather than hurt them. In the end, it's about putting them behind bars so they don't do it again."

"You're right, but I don't know if I could do it, especially with kids." I twirled the piny air freshener he had over his rear-view mirror.

"Yeah, that's tough, too. But it's all the same premise."

On our final drive home, I asked, "Wanna stay in touch?"

"Sure." He double-parked in front of my apartment.

"Okay, great. Thanks for all the rides, the coffees, doughnuts, and most of all, the talks."

"You're welcome. Thank you, too." He smiled.

"It was nice talking to someone intelligent and openminded," I added.

He nodded. "Same here. I know what you mean. Be safe."

"You, safer. Remember, I'm in Sussex." I leaned back to grab my purse and notebook.

He laughed. "That's right."

It wasn't the last time we saw each other.

A week later, my sergeant called out, "Julia?"

Having finished eating a turkey sandwich at my desk, I headed to his office. The wooden floors in the old, undisclosed two-story house we used as our base for narcotics operations creaked.

"Yes, Sergeant?"

He replaced his telephone in its cradle. "That was Lakewood Special Ops. Come in. They want you to do some undercover work for them. You can go, but I told them they can only have you for seven days: four days the first week, three the next." He paused.

"When do I begin?"

"July 27, when you're back from A.T. Give them a call." He handed me a message slip. "The detective's name is Jon Tillwater. He'll tell you where to report. They're paying for your lodging and meals. Good luck, Julia."

"Thank you." I could've shouted with glee. There was a week left before I went with my reserve unit to our two-week annual training in Fort Dix, New Jersey, and then I'd get some excitement.

Back at my desk, I dialed Jon's number, and we agreed on a time and place to meet for my assignment.

I went home that night and called Rick. "Let's celebrate!"

"You're *going*, huh?" He was as excited as me.

"I told you. Come on, hurry up and come get me."

"Okay, okay. Give me fifteen."

I rushed out of my apartment. When I saw his black Saab pull around the corner, I flagged him down and threw myself in it.

"Hey, catch your breath," he said, smiling.

"I'm *sooo* happy."

"Yeah, I see that. Ice cream okay?"

"Sure. We can eat it by 80<sup>th</sup> Street Park."

"Sounds good."

Before you knew it, we were sitting in his car, eating chocolate and vanilla ice cream in cups.

"Listen, J.," he began, concern in his eyes clear. "I'm really happy for you, but are you gonna be all right?"

"You mean the baby?" I asked, savoring the chocolate scoop.

"Yeah—I mean, this is gonna be your first time."

"I know, but we'll be fine." I rubbed my small belly, glancing at the swings where toddlers shouted in glee.

There was a vital factor to consider—the CO's five-year pregnancy warning in the Gulf—but it hadn't crossed my mind.

"Do they know?" he asked.

"No, only the military. I'm restricted from being near the gas chamber. You know that's what I teach, it wouldn't be good. It may seem irresponsible, but I don't wanna say anything until I'm showing. It's not like I'll be doing daredevil stuff. I'm just gonna be buying off street dealers."

"I know, but I worry about you. What about the baby's dad?"

"After he said he'd be supportive, he began to hesitate when a friend questioned it, so I told him not to call me. Now he calls Rose, you know, my old college friend, to check up on me."

"Because he cares." The Mr. Softee ice cream truck pulled over near Rick; its whimsical tune brought a group of teenagers.

I shook my head. "No, because he feels guilty. I like him, but if he's gonna believe his friend over me, then I don't want him. I won't try to change his mind. He's a grown man, and by the way, I don't even like his last name."

"What is it?"

"Pupo."

He laughed.

"It sounds like poop," I said.

He roared, almost spilling ice cream on his jeans. "You didn't tell him that, did you?"

"Not the poop part, but I did tell him I didn't like it. Why wouldn't I? And I also made it clear that I didn't want or need anything from him, nor did I have an ulterior motive. I said I was only telling him 'cause he was the dad and he had a right to know."

"You're right, but be careful, okay? If you need anything, page me." He finished his cup and tossed both in a garbage can.

My friendship with Rick had indeed evolved, but I wouldn't know how great a man he was until a few weeks later, when a devastating event unexpectedly altered a few lives.